THE WAY OF BACH

THE WAY

OF

THE WAY OF *Bach*

THREE YEARS WITH THE MAN,
THE MUSIC, AND THE PIANO

Dan Moller

PEGASUS BOOKS
NEW YORK LONDON

THE WAY OF BACH

Pegasus Books, Ltd.
148 W 37th Street, 13th Floor
New York, NY 10018

First Pegasus Books cloth edition November 2020

Bach monogram by Valerii Baryshpolets,
loosely following Bach's own designs.

The BWV 847 manuscript appears
courtesy of the Staatsbibliothek zu Berlin.
https://digital.staatsbibliothek-berlin.de
/werkansicht/?PPN=PPN813072077.

Interior design by Maria Fernandez

ISBN: 978-1-64313-580-9

10 9 8 7 6 5 4 3 2 1

Printed in the United States of America
Distributed by Simon & Schuster
www.pegasusbooks.com

Contents

THE WAY OF BACH

Preface

T he aim in what follows is not to teach the reader how to play Bach, nor to offer a formal introduction to his life and work. I am a lousy if enthusiastic piano player, and thus unqualified to offer instruction, and I lack the expertise of a historian or musicologist. Aspiring pianists should, if anything, learn from my mistakes, and historians and musicologists will want to denounce my haphazard approach, which is driven by intensely personal likes and dislikes—the minor keys good, the major keys bad, the harpsichord even worse, etc.

What I have tried to convey in this book is rather the felt *experience* of an adult learning Bach, from the point of view of someone who *loves* Bach with a completely unprofessional, undetached abandon, and I have tried to explain that feeling in terms of his life and work. My greatest hope for this little diary is that it might inspire one or two people to take up the piano, or recall some musical apostates to the faith.

Music referenced can be found as a playlist at www.dan moller.org.

ONE

The Bug

The desire to play Bach came to me one night in June like a sickness. Or rather, that was the night that the sickness became too much to bear, and I knew that I must simply yield to it, the way those mortally injured eventually close their eyes and find peace in death.

I had tried to learn to play Bach years before, in school, but had utterly failed because of a repetitive strain injury. I decided that listening was enough and that I would find other "creative outlets," which is to say that I yielded to temptation and fear and gave up. But by then I was already infected even if I didn't know it yet, and there was no cure. In fact, from the time I heard the first Fugue in C minor from *The Well-Tempered Clavier* at seventeen, there was always going to be some night of reckoning, some crucible of the soul in which I would have to make my choice.

What was it about that fugue? I didn't even know what the word meant, much less what tempering was, or how to do it well. And in fact, that fugue is far from Bach's best, as I came to see. It lacks the awesome complexity of his later works, featuring only three distinct voices, two of which move in parallel, and few of the ingenious devices the form permits. (On the other hand, the melodic lines are invertible—you can flip the bottom or middle line to the top and vice versa, which is no mean feat.) An experienced ear would group it with the accomplished but hardly brilliant middle-period works, not in the same class as what Bach produced in the last ten years of his life. It is better, we might say, than almost anything written by his contemporaries, but workmanlike by his own ultimate standards. Perhaps it was its very brusqueness that gripped me as a sullen teenager. I couldn't relate to the gilded parlors of Venice and Vivaldi, or the music of Versailles—I was from the Boston suburbs; I wore flip-flops and T-shirts. But *this* music, written by an organist glowering in his stony aerie? Well, that made some sense to me. Salem wasn't very far; we read peevish Puritans like Hawthorne in English class, and I sensed a connection.

Listening before I knew what to listen for, that fugue reminded me more of Metallica than the classical music I had heard up till then. The staccato rhythms had an edge that sounded nothing like the tinkly snuffbox that was classical radio. There was an insistence in those sixteenth notes, a frustration that was being worked out. But above all there was that glorious *riff* that opened the piece and then returned again and again, just like Metallica's "Four Horsemen" or "Seek & Destroy." The texture was thick and complicated, full of activity and substance. I sensed that there were multiple ideas being developed at once, that there were currents rushing beneath the surface in every direction. And yet all of that drama seemed contained and controlled; it wasn't bombastic screeching from Italian opera nor the sentimental mush of a Romantic composer. Nor, on the other hand, was it elegant and perfect like the little Mozart confections I remembered from childhood; there was that roughness. But it was the roughness that can make us enjoy the less mature work of a master, still charged with fury and youth, more than his serene masterpieces. T. S. Eliot may have preferred his later ramblings about time and space, but I liked the bite of the early "Prufrock," the comic rage of a man whose life was measured out in coffee spoons.

The normal thing to do at that point would have been to seek out a piano teacher. But being a teacher myself, I had come to form a deep loathing for teachers of all sorts, for pedagogy in general, and for music teachers in particular.

Teachers, I found, were usually the chief obstacle to learning anything, or at least they prevented getting any enjoyment out of learning, which was the prerequisite to learning more. Professors resent their students because they stand in the way of writing the obscure articles that lead to academic glory; conservatory-trained musicians teach only when they cannot make music for a living. And once these teachers are reduced to a life of Sisyphus, of endlessly correcting childish mistakes, they lose all joy in their subject matter. Why, that past semester I had corrected plenty of my own students' sentences, the most impressive of which read, "We must never falter on our beliefs, and crumple at the hands of the opposer," which was so very odd, so mystically strange, that I took to incanting it throughout the day as a kind of prayer. In fact, the only thing worse than teachers are students. They quickly forget why they are studying to begin with and succumb to sloth and distraction, which causes their teachers to adopt a warden mentality, which reinforces the pupils' resistance, and so on, in a downward vortex that ends only in the nirvana of summer.

The other problem with the piano teachers was that they would have their own ideas about what to play. I had no interest in playing anything but Bach. Perhaps, in the very distant future, I could imagine attempting Ravel or Debussy, whom I liked, or transcriptions of Wagner, but I doubted I would ever be good enough. And in the meantime, the thought of being tortured through the normal repertoire terrified me. The piano teacher's goal is to make the student proficient at playing the piano, but I had no desire to be a good pianist. What I wanted was to play *Bach*. Only Bach. On the piano. A certain general facility for the instrument was inevitable, but I couldn't bear to spend years trudging through workbooks of children's songs and exercises, especially having reached my forties, and then on to the warhorses of Mozart, Beethoven, and Chopin.

I was confused by how other people thought about this. Why should it be important to have a general competence at the instrument? The reply from music lovers, and especially conservatory-trained teachers, was that the music composed for the instrument was generally worthwhile. But I did not share this appraisal. In fact, I was deeply suspicious of anyone who liked classical music *in general*, as if dinner *in general* tasted good, or old stuff written in books was *generally* worthwhile. People resent the opinionated, but all true lovers are fiercely discriminating. On the contrary, I found hardly any music worthwhile. Pop music had become an algorithmic pablum, cynically marketed as a lifestyle product, and the classical repertoire was full of pompous nose-blowers like Beethoven, it seemed to me, or lightweights like Rossini. In fact, even within Bach, many of his works were of no interest to me—those faceless cantatas, the period of his "Italian captivity," and on and on. But his great works—*The Well-Tempered Clavier*, *The Goldberg Variations*, *The Art of Fugue*, the keyboard partitas, the

St Matthew Passion, the Chaconne from the Partita in D Minor, the cello suites, and many others—each of these merited a lifetime of devotion in itself.

I knew how to read some music from noodling around with guitar in high school, and I had a friend, Christopher, who had been to a conservatory. Plus, there was the Internet. Did I really need a teacher? How hard could it be? It was true that Christopher still lived in Boston while I had moved to Maryland, that he had dropped out of the conservatory and had been a composition major in any case, but no matter. He could play Mozart's Rondo Alla Turca at twice the normal tempo! That was all the teacher I needed.

I came to the conclusion that I would give an arm, or at least a few toes, for the piano. This wasn't just a cliché: I genuinely believed it would be worth sacrificing a limb to be able to play, and in a sense I did.

I had tried to learn to play the piano back in graduate school, around the time Mother's cancer returned. At first I thought I was making tremendous strides; clearly I was a brilliant autodidact. It all seemed fairly easy, and soon I was practicing for hours, when I wasn't working at my laptop. But after a few months I started to develop a debilitating neural disorder; a strange discomfort—not exactly pain in the normal sense—swept up and down my forearms and into my right hand. Playing the keyboard and working on my laptop both seemed to aggravate the symptoms. I tried taking a few days off, then a week, but nothing seemed to help. After gouging my arms with needles, a neurologist confirmed that there was a nerve conductivity problem. A surgeon then offered a diagnosis of carpal tunnel syndrome after ten minutes of examination and proposed surgery, which accomplished nothing at all, just like Mother's chemotherapy, besides leaving me helpless in bandages for several weeks. A year after starting, I gave up playing with the greatest dejection. My German grandmother enthusiastically proclaimed that I *deserved* this for having developed the wrong technique without a teacher—what pride! what hubris!—and for a while I was inclined to agree. But after ten years away from the piano, things had not improved much. My hands both caught fire occasionally and gave me strange neuralgic symptoms, as if someone were tapping on a thousand funny bones up and down my arms. Some days I couldn't hold a fork. It seemed that this soft injury had canceled my rendezvous with Bach.

But that summer night, heaving about, trying not to wake Lauren, I decided that I simply could not accept this result: it was entirely unacceptable. I said this to myself in the spirit that one might announce that something long settled in the past was "unacceptable," even when it isn't up to us, as if the Gallic wars or a death in the family were unacceptable. I would either play Bach or die trying. The prospect of making another attempt filled me with dread, though. Failing again would be unbearable, as would another round with useless doctors who spent ten or fifteen minutes with me only to offer some casual misdiagnosis. These vague, soft-tissue ailments appeared to be unknowable. Doctors would pronounce when asked, but these pronouncements proceeded not from knowledge but from the pressure to *do* something. If you must be injured, for heaven's sake break an arm or poke out an eye—these they know how to deal with; everything else and it might as well be leeches.

I owed my eventual healing to American hucksterism. I began, lying in bed that summer night, by reflecting on what I would pay to be able to play once again. The answer, I found, was more or less anything. Certainly, I would happily have paid $60,000, say, for a fancy surgery that guaranteed success. But then it occurred to me that for the same sum I could hire someone for an entire year to do nothing but research how to solve this problem. Better yet, I could offer ⅔ the amount up front and the rest as a bonus in case of improvement. Since I knew I did many foolish things that made my problems worse, it seemed to me this could work. But after tossing and turning some more, I realized that there was nothing my medical adviser could tell me that I didn't already know deep down, or couldn't easily find out. An imaginary adviser would do quite as well as the real thing, as long as I followed his fictitious directives. A simple heuristic presented itself: pretend to have such a counselor, and then do whatever he said.

It came to me that my adviser would immediately order me to do all kinds of mundane things to fix my workspace. He would tell me to get rid of my armchair that prevented decent posture and invited reclining, which placed more pressure on my forearms. He would make me stop using a laptop. He would tell me to stop spending all day at my workstation, to stop fiddling with my phone incessantly, and a million similar, trivial things. He would buy me every book about repetitive strain problems, he would get me an electric massager to apply to my forearms, he would enforce a stretching regime.

One by one, I began doing these. Individually, each seemed futile and I would never have done them on my own. But my imaginary friend kept reminding me of what I had sworn—that I would follow each of his instructions to the letter—and so I felt compelled to follow through, like King Darius who had a servant remind him three times a day to smite the Greeks. I researched voice dictation methods. They were all terrible, and everything took ten times longer than before, but I used them anyway. When they didn't work I just typed with one hand, even though I was writing a book. If I balked at anything my adviser grabbed me by the lapels and screamed, covering me in spit, "Do you want to play Bach or not?" Shamed, I would yield. And that is how I gave my right arm to play Bach, like a character in one of those creepy fairy tales from Andersen or Grimm that Disney must bowdlerize to suit the American psyche.

Perhaps it wasn't even Bach I was attracted to, so much as the musical form known as fugue, which Bach happened to write better than anyone else. A fugue consists of a kind of conversation between several voices, some speaking in a higher and others in a lower register. The first speaker announces the theme or subject of the conversation while the others sit still and listen. Then the next voice takes over, repeating the subject, while the first moves on to other matters. Eventually, there is a great roaring murmur kept in order by the strict rules each speaker must follow and by the recurring subject, which keeps passing from voice to voice, like a game at a party in which someone must always be discussing Marilyn Monroe.

Initially, I could recognize only that opening riff in the Fugue in C Minor, which was the first to grip me. It wasn't what one would call pretty the way Mozart or Vivaldi are pretty, in a singsong kind of way. The theme was compact, to the point, like a muscle car or a cut gemstone, and the combination of short and long tones lent an emphasis to certain notes which gave the whole a propulsive, head-banging quality. Because the subject was announced naked at the outset, even newcomers could recognize it in different registers throughout, returning ever anew but slightly altered in form and pitch, familiar but alarming, like a lover who returns from the war with a glass eye and fondles you with his prosthetic limb.

Meanwhile, once that first subject had dropped off, its line continued in an animated patter that maintained the impression of a single voice pressing onward, until the next voice, a soprano, took over the stage, until she too sank beneath the surface, making way for the bass, and all three voices were heard, one after the other making his or her brash entry on the initial theme, before submerging once again. The effect was one of wave after wave crashing over me.

I didn't understand much of what happened after this expository phase; I simply delighted in waiting for those waves to come rolling back around. The repetition appealed to me, since it offered more of a foothold. Pop songs have simple trajectories that are instantly accessible, but symphonies repeat their themes rather less, and they're harder to distinguish and follow as they're recombined and developed. The rest of the fugue remained indistinct, a mesmerizing texture that was impenetrable, like Islamic tile art in Granada or Cordoba. What I could hear was simply that those three voices continued ever onward, murmuring to one another in a pattern that seemed inscrutably complex. Even this I liked, however. The sound was absolute. No one was imitating a bird or trying to evoke some pat love story. Each note spoke for itself and conveyed its own meaning.

Later, I began to hear a bit more. Listening to a fugue was like staring at those Islamic tessellations for an extended time. At first they deflect the eye, before we come to grasp their structure and design. We start out seeing only one or two elements, but gradually we notice how these interlock and then form up to suggest greater wholes, which in turn make up patterns of their own. I began to notice episodes in between the entries of the subject. These episodes seemed to snap off bits and pieces of the main theme, to vary and realign them, and then sequence them as if with a synthesizer, so that the fragment was repeated at rising pitches, creating more and more tension, until the subject came crashing through again, like a rogue wave.

In the beginning, I only paid attention to recognizing the melodies. But once I grew accustomed to them, harmonies and scales began to emerge as well, albeit crudely at first. There was the key that the C minor fugue opened with, which I liked, and then later there was the dreaded major key, which sounded happy but insipid. Christopher told me that I was a drama queen and a misanthrope for hating the major and wanting to hear only sad music, but that was only partly true. Major and minor are ways of dividing up musical space, like stations on a rail line, and they aren't the only ones. French impressionists like Debussy and folk music like "Amazing Grace" use other systems that sound perfectly happy and yet didn't bother me at all. The problem with the major wasn't its superficial mood connotations, but something about the exact positioning of the railway stops, which drove me crazy.

Nevertheless, there was something charming about Bach's modulations from major to minor and back again in these fugues, in the changes in key, and even in the major. The difference lay in what these changes accomplished and what their role seemed to be. The goal was to present already familiar material in a fresh light, to reveal new facets of music we thought we knew backward and forward. When the theme of a minor key fugue suddenly announces itself in the major, we are jolted from complacency, forced to reexamine all of our assumptions, like a painter who depicts the familiar from a fresh perspective—Monet's gothic cathedrals, which are depicted not as hunchbacks but all summer and light.

To most people I knew, this music sounded quite mechanical and lifeless. The pacing was constant and there weren't any fortissimos to rouse us; an elaborate set of rules governed everything that happened, which ruled out spontaneity. But as I listened to the C Minor for the twentieth, for the fiftieth time, it seemed to me as thrilling as any hit tune, only composed in an idiom we find harder to understand now, and at a miniature scale we struggle to make out. The noise of the drum machine, the speed of the Internet deaden us to an older sense of proportion that we must rediscover with a little effort. Part of the problem is that these fugues in *The Well-Tempered Clavier* are often intended to contrast with the unruly preludes they're paired with, and yet we often hear them detached or fail to notice this opposition: first come the drunken maenads of Dionysus, then the stately procession of Apollo. Ignoring the one and then declaring the other lifeless is like complaining about the absence of sorbet on your steak.

⁂

I started fooling around at the keyboard. Each morning was a mock execution as I waited for my hand problems to resurface. There were all kinds of minor aches and pains as I got used to playing, and each of these made me fear the end. It sounds absurd, but taking up the piano was the scariest thing I did in my life, even if this is mainly a testament to my milquetoast. If I failed again, how would I go on? Perhaps it was better not to try. I told myself that if I could only play a few measures a day, it would be worth it, but I knew on some level that this wasn't true, that it would be the greatest torment of all. A philosophy professor would probably say: "If you fail, you won't be any worse off than you already are, and if you succeed, you will have gained something of great value," but then that's why people don't really like philosophers very much. The problem was in the accounting. I had already taken a charge for not being able to play—my emotional stock had taken its hit—and I was back on my treadmill hamstering away. Playing again meant a whole new investment, another set of possible losses and bankruptcy.

Since it was unclear to me whether I would be able to play much at all, I began practicing on a synth keyboard with weighted keys. But obviously this was no good in the long run. And I began to suspect that it may have contributed to my hand problems, since the keys were narrow and a bit sticky and didn't really feel like a mechanical device at all. It was time to buy a real instrument. And yet if I bought a big, expensive piano and it turned out I was unable to play it because after seven months my hands fell off my arms, I would feel even worse, stuck with that great coffin filling the room. An obvious solution was to buy a modest upright to tuck away in a corner someplace, at least until I could see how things were going. But the keyboard action of an upright piano felt all wrong to me. When you depress an upright key, you aren't counteracting gravity but a spring; the feel is completely different and totally inimical to rapid, baroque-style ornaments, or so I had determined from trying one or two at random for a few minutes. And, I reasoned, getting a fancy piano would shame me into practicing, and compel me to do whatever it took to stay healthy.

But behind these reasons, there lay my sheer fascination with the grand piano itself—its voluptuous beauty, the curves of John Singer Sargent's *Madame X*, the elaborate keyboard mechanism, and of course its sound, which I had come to associate with good music in general. Oddly, I loved Bach and the way he sounded on the piano, but I hated the Baroque and anything that sounded Baroque, and above all the harpsichord—oh God, not the harpsichord! The moment I heard that metallic clanging, the thin rattling of a child tinkling into a jar, I reached for the off button. It sounded like musty old wigs and the wrong ideas of the past. That sound was perfectly appropriate to old composers in wigs whose ideas *were* in fact wrong, like Telemann, whose mediocre essence was transmitted quite adequately by recorders and the harpsichord, but not to Bach. The piano, by contrast, had a clarity, a neutrality that gave whatever was performed on it a timeless quality that Bach deserved. His best music isn't bound to a period, to frilly architecture and gaudy decor; it is more like the Parthenon or *Pietà*, a possession for all time. The piano is the instrument of eternity; the harpsichord belongs in some garish museum at Versailles. Purists want to dig up the original, rusting instruments to play, but the authenticity that matters lies in *how* you play. Playing Bach on the keytar is perfectly acceptable when done with precision and verve, while all the period hardware in the world won't save a saccharine performance.

I made my way to the local piano warehouse, and was amazed at my good fortune: everything was on sale! And now a new set of terrors emerged, since there was the humiliating need to try out pianos in front of an audience of salesmen, musicians, and backroom tuners. I could barely play anything, just a few fragments I couldn't resist learning right away, and I could only just stumble through those. I tried to find an obscure corner to begin with, but the moment I began playing, all of the tuners working in the back stopped what they were doing, evidently to listen to me. I tried to play softly, pawing at the keys with sweaty fingers. The keys felt stiff, the tone was spotlight bright, and the construction rattly, even for a used instrument. $15,000 for this?

Eventually a salesman loomed into view, a shifty, seedy hornswoggling type, who insisted this was the piano for me. He asked if I was practicing Hanon's exercises, which he sat down and proceeded to play. I tried to look knowledgeable, at least as knowledgeable as someone completely ignorant can look, and I asked about the age of the piano, the method of construction, and so on. Eventually I made it clear that I didn't require further assistance, and he left in something of a huff. I moved to the next piano, and the next, and the next, and the next. Eventually one sounded right, even if it cost too much and seemed to date back to the Empire of Japan, which is where it was made. The action was punchy, and the tone worn in and velvety, like the patina on a cozy sofa. It was a couple of inches longer than I was, it had a middle pedal, which I only vaguely registered at the time, but later was desperately grateful for, and it could be delivered the next week. When it came time for the upsell, I could muster only faint resistance, and I wound up with a complicated moisture-control system that required me to water my piano like a needy plant.

When the great day came, I rushed to clear out the room and make way in the hall. The movers expressed a great deal of confidence that melted away once they were in the process of getting the piano through a series of narrow hairpin turns that required gymnastic contortions. They only succeeded by fractions of an inch, but there it was: a great hulking raven, pinion fully fledged and ready for flight, whatever my poor ministrations and however small the room.

With fear and trembling I bought some books and began learning to read music and to handle the keyboard. I started to study the bass staff—the bottom set of lines in piano notation—which was entirely unfamiliar to me, and tried to remember how to read the treble clef. Musical notation seemed deeply beautiful to me quite apart from what it stood for. The beams swooped across the page, dropping stems as from a fruit tree, met by interlocking notes ascending from below, occasionally arrested by swirls declaring a halt, or sainted with the halo of a staccato-dot. It was a language that suggested both rigor and grace. Everywhere were discontinuities and ruled lines that set out boundaries to respect, but the slurs arced like the hem on a ballroom dress, and the note heads themselves danced at an angle.

It seemed like an eternity before I could connect what was written on the pages of the music desk with the machinery below, or even remember which keys corresponded to which notes. And the further I strayed from the safety of the staves, the tougher things got. It was easy to remember that the bottommost line represented G, but it was harder to recognize the notes perched on the short lines extending ladder-like below. And the physical gap between the sheet music and the keyboard was its own problem. The music desk was set at an elevation that encouraged correct posture, but which also prevented you from seeing your hands and the music at the same time, so that the beginner was forced to switch awkwardly back and forth. I was fretful of never managing the transition to looking simply at the music, to developing an automatic sense of where my hands were in relation to the keys, so I tried my best to feel for the notes, fumbling by the 2-3 pattern of black keys as if fishing for gum in my pocket. Whenever I glanced down, I had the vertiginous sense of dangling from a great height.

All of these mundane problems were humiliating. I, who dreamt in counterpoint and agonized over the one true recording of the *The Goldberg Variations*—I couldn't remember which note this blob of ink referred to, or how to get through "Twinkle, Twinkle, Little Star." It was disorienting to be lost in a domain so intuitive to me from listening, like someone learning his letters as an adult. And this feeling only grew stronger when the material I practiced proved to be so insipid. Of course, beginners can't play much, but my beginner's book seemed to be premised on wanting to become some sort of honky-tonk specialist, or perhaps a colonial ethnographer; it was bad enough that I was reduced to pecking out tunes, but now

I, who had five recordings of *The Art of Fugue*, was reduced to pecking out "Mexican Hat Dance #3."

Meanwhile, on every other page there was a theory lesson, introducing the reader to scales, intervals, chords, inversions, chord progressions, cadences, rhythmic devices, and the like. Working on these felt like working through my sixth grade reading worksheets; I half expected nap time and a glass of milk to follow. On the other hand, it was exhilarating finally to grasp the underlying structures that I had felt or sensed for so many years without explicitly understanding, so that I could start hearing all those additional layers in the C Minor fugue. An octave corresponded to a doubling in frequency, which was the number of sound waves per second. The major scale was annoying because of how stupid that particular way of traipsing through the octave was.

Learning the piano as an adult thus aroused two distinct and opposed feelings. One was the sense of absurdity in trudging through these puerile exercises as a grownup, in the recognition that I was decades behind—an enlightened four-year-old would have been far ahead of me. St. Augustine observed, in his un-American way, that any sane person would rather die than go through childhood again, and I could only agree, working through my hat dance. But on the other hand, there was the joy of insight that would have been impossible until I was an adult—the epiphany that all music was based on dividing the octave according to a particular pattern, that tonal music was based on patterns of stable and unstable harmonies—as well as the motivation actually to *do* what would have had to have been flogged into me as a child. As it was, I couldn't wait to rise in the morning and practice before going to work. In childhood, the technique necessary to appreciate anything must usually be acquired at the same pace as the appreciation itself, while the grownup has at least this advantage, that he can fall in love before he must practice writing his sonnets.

I began to study Bach on the piano because I wanted to participate in the greatness of it, to become a part of the music itself. T. S. Eliot, in those later ramblings, speaks of music heard so deeply that you *are* the music, intending a figure of speech. But in playing an instrument you really can get close to being, or at least realizing the music, since you are the one creating the sounds. Your fingers are the vehicle through which the composer resurrects the body of his work and his music becomes incarnate; for a moment your hands are his hands. When you play Bach, there is a sense in which *he* is playing *you*, even long after he is dead, a sense in which you are one more complication of his keyboard, one more distant gear to engage.

In this, music is quite different from painting, where we can but distantly admire the greatness, say, of Manet's *Bar at the Folies-Bergère*, without any hope of becoming a part of it—on the contrary, its vitality only serves to highlight how passive we are as venerants trembling before it. Literature is no better, since it, too, runs along fixed tracks; perhaps only acting and dance can compare. Music lets you plug into the composer himself, to have his power and personality rip through you, which was part of what made it so unbearable to play anyone other than Bach, since it was like having someone unworthy inhabit your very body, to occupy your own hands like an unwilling glove; and conversely, in playing the tiny fragments of Bach that I had learned, for a few brief instants I felt myself channel all that was good in the world. I set myself the task over the next few years to play, if not master, the Fugue in C Minor.

It was with the utmost despair, then, that I woke up after the first week of practice, and felt a numb, tingling sensation proceeding from my elbow down through my forearm. I got out of bed and tried shaking it out, but without success. I showered and worked my forearms with the electric massager I had bought, I stretched carefully, but nothing worked: there was a quivering weakness in my arms that made them useless to play. I sank my head into my arms at that big, expensive coffin and wept.

2

The Music

W hy Bach? There were the individual pieces that moved me, but there was also something deeper. It wasn't that I admired his work in general—the suspicious creed of the indiscriminate and therefore undiscerning. But there was something about the pieces I did prize that made them stand apart even from the masterpieces of other composers. The something, it turned out, was counterpoint.

If a fugue is a conversation that examines a particular subject, counterpoint is the conversation itself, the very fact of overlapping voices, each speaking separately but in sync. In music, what a voice says is its melody, and since it is written left to right on the page, we can think of it as moving horizontally. But if many voices are speaking at once, there is also the harmony (or dissonance) of the conversation at any one time, which gives music a vertical dimension, as well. These are the chords spelled out by the notes we hear overlapping in a given moment. And the fundamental problem is that these two dimensions often conflict: a complex, interesting melody tends to be more difficult to layer on top of other complex melodies without turning into noise, and if you have thick chords with many voices stacked on top of one another it becomes more difficult to keep up separate melodies. Any of us can hum a decent tune, and some of us could harmonize a second alongside, but few could add a third or a fourth without the whole thing breaking down.

There are several ways of resolving this tension. Renaissance composers like Palestrina or Thomas Tallis favored dense, lush compositions—Tallis's *Spem in alium* is scored for *forty* voices—but at the cost of punchy melodies; the sound is serene but mushy and contains nothing you are likely to whistle to yourself later. Classical composers like the Mozart of *Eine kleine Nachtmusik*, on the other hand, produced intensely vivid lines that sound as if they were etched in glass, but these lines are often sad and lonely, supported by vertical chords that act as columns holding up the main line rather than supplying independent ideas. (The same is true of folk or rock guitar, whose chords are strummed in blocks that sustain the central melody.) The Renaissance approach can be described as polyphony, since it consists of a great many (poly) sounds (phony), while the classical approach is homophonic, since the sounds all support the same, unitary line.

The counterpoint of Bach seeks to unite the best in each, despite the fact that the one emerged before and the other only blossomed after Bach's time. In the literal sense, his music is polyphonic, like a Renaissance composition, since there are many sounds at once, but counterpoint seeks to harmonize lines that are each, in the ideal, as dramatic and memorable as one of Mozart's catchy tunes. The effect is of an impossible coincidence, as if four artists made separate paintings which, when superimposed, somehow produced a coherent whole you would never have predicted from the individual canvases. Of course, it isn't really a coincidence, and the appearance of independently conceived melodies that just happen to stack up is in part artifice and illusion. But that is its glory. It shouldn't be possible to heap melody after melody on top of one another without devolving into chaos, but that is what the art of counterpoint accomplishes.

"If it's really that hard, then how come so many musicians manage to do it? There must be a trick." There are certainly tricks, shortcuts, conventions. Avoid parallel fifths, don't cross lines. The very constraints inherent in the rules of counterpoint are, in another sense, advantages, since they clarify the composer's options. But in fact, very few musicians *do* make an effort at counterpoint. They don't stumble over the difficulties since they never really try. Instead, they either play simple melodies with light accompaniment to fill out the harmony, or thick chords whose constituent notes don't make up intelligible melodies in their own right, or they go back and forth between the notes making up such chords. There are occasional exceptions. The band sings a harmony, some jazz soloists improvise over one another. But these rarely involve complex melodies moving independently for an extended time; by and large, counterpoint has come to be seen as an aberration, a stylistic feature of a few particular periods, a gesture that makes us perk up and say, "Ah, the Baroque," or "Ah, Beethoven is trying to write a fugue again."

But as I delved into Bach, I came to reject this point of view. Counterpoint isn't just another style, and adopting it isn't optional. Or rather, ignoring polyphony (in the broad sense) is like painting in monochrome—there are legitimate reasons for doing so, but they're exotic, hardly the default. The point of music, I found myself screaming at Christopher during our late-night Schubertiads—the *point* of music (are we out of Scotch?) is to harmonize melodies, not that he seriously disagreed. Its specific virtue is precisely that it allows us to represent several ideas at once, to hold multiple conversations that overlap, to double, triple, and quadruple our conscious experience in a way that shouldn't be possible. There is an almost theological difference between those who think of music vertically ("Listen to those chords!"), those who think of it horizontally ("What a tune!"), and those who think in terms of counterpoint. Counterpoint is the musical approach to music.

In time, the tingling in my arms receded, and I was able to begin playing again, albeit always with a sense of dread. In the morning, as soon as I awoke I stretched out my arms and inspected them on the way to the shower, as if assessing an unreliable piece of equipment. There were bad days and worse. Sometimes I could only play fifteen minutes; on other occasions I could manage an hour spread across several sessions. My forearms often felt exhausted, as if I had been lifting weights, even as I was careful to limit playing time, employ good form, stretch, and use the massager.

Christopher refused to believe that my problem could be anything other than a character flaw, a lack of moral fiber. In our phone calls we went over and over a checklist of possible mistakes. Was my seat adjusted properly? Were my fingers loosely gripping the "ball"? Was I secretly trying to play the "Emperor" Concerto? These friendly suspicions reminded me of Lauren's case, since she had—strangely—developed her own musical disabilities which mimicked mine, and which in my worse moments I questioned impatiently. Tribulations for which we don't want to muster the sympathy must be the victim's fault, we like to suppose, thereby letting ourselves off the hook.

I learned to be strategic about when I practiced, to distribute sessions across the course of the day, so that I practiced in the morning, in the evening when I came home, and then again before going to bed, to maximize recovery time. I took Sundays off altogether. I practiced more intensely before leaving on a trip, knowing there would be many days to get better. But I didn't seem to be making much progress: my arms seemed unwilling to accept that playing the piano was a perfectly natural, unambitious task; apparently at random, my arms—mostly the right—would become too sore to play.

When this happened, I tried to carry on with my left arm, working at least to improve on reading music and playing figures in the bass. I thought of these as my Wittgenstein days, after the philosopher Ludwig Wittgenstein's brother Paul, who lost an arm in the First World War but kept on playing, including the concerto for (just) the left hand that he commissioned from Ravel. Wittgenstein moved me greatly. The world is independent of our will, but we can still assert it as far as it will go. Surely it would have been easier simply to give up than to make fanatical efforts to play on with just one hand, to learn Ravel's mediocre concerto, to suffer the inevitable qualifications of the reviewers ("Not bad for a one-armed gimp!"). If he lost the other arm would he have continued playing with his nose perhaps, telling visitors it was just a flesh wound, or that it was nothing compared to what his Jewish family, the richest in Europe, had to give the Nazis in order to survive?

Still, I had reached the point where playing was a viable activity. Even with all of the interruptions and Wittgenstein days, the process was sustainable and I was making forward progress. The very concept of progress in this domain came as a revelation. At first I dismissed it as mere wishful thinking, but eventually there was no denying it: before I could not play "Mexican Hat Dance #3," now I could. Things could get better. I took heart in the infinite difference between a trajectory that was perfectly level, incapable of change, and one directed ever so slightly upward from the horizon, which could take you as high as you liked, if only you continued far enough.

This thought carried me through days sitting at my desk correcting papers, wishing desperately I could be at the piano. On a long enough timeline success was inevitable, I reflected, even as I struck out a student's phrase—No, not "Descartes's *Mediations*." Eventually I would get home. Eventually I would finish dinner and sit down at the piano and practice—No, not "his septical philosophy"—eventually I would play that Fugue in C Minor.

As I eased back into practicing, I revisited some of Bach's masterpieces with a newfound curiosity about their technique, and what each had to say about counterpoint.

I began with *The Well-Tempered Clavier*, a mid-period work whose title is forbidding—more antiquarian than sexy—but whose structure is vivid and inviting. Bach tours each of the twelve major and minor keys from C major to B minor and offers us a prelude and fugue in each. He then loops back around and does it again in *Book II*, in a process that took him many years and which involved collecting and assembling disparate pieces he often seems to have composed for other occasions. Plainly, exploring this cycle meant a great deal to him. The reason for this was that Bach was demonstrating that by fudging the tuning of the keyboard just a little—that is what tempering means—you can modulate freely from key to key, which isn't possible if you tune according to what mathematical perfection would suggest. The idea wasn't original to Bach, but this tour through all the key signatures made it seem obvious and compelling, and showed there was no going back. *The Well-Tempered Clavier* thus aims to charm us note by note, but also to make a grander, more philosophical point, which I found to be true of much of Bach's music.

Circling from key to key, it became clear that counterpoint needn't be rigid or stultifying despite the complex rules that keep all those voices in check. One might suppose that fugues in such a long series as twenty-four must eventually seem dull, especially when the basic structure—the statement of the subject, the exposition, the various episodes, and the rest—is largely fixed. But the variety of styles and techniques Bach employs makes us forget we are listening to one essential form. The Fugue in D Major in *Book I* is a French pastry puff, all gestures of light; the opening notes shimmy across the keyboard in a flourish, and the other voices join in just for fun. Dotted notes hop and skip like dancers at court, and the contrasts between the flourishes and the languorous dotted notes whirl us in ever faster circles around the ballroom. The style has its origin in a pompous overture for the king, but this is the orchestra making merry after the king has passed out and been carried to bed. And yet just before, in the preceding Fugue in C-sharp Minor, we languished in darkness. There, we find not just three, or four, but *five* distinct voices intertwined, and not one, or two, but *three* distinct themes—a triple fugue. The opening is as slow and dismal as its successor is bright, and the atmosphere is German and Lutheran to its core; the opening notes even form the outline of a cross.

By contrast, the endless variety of forms in the preludes might suggest a certain randomness, since few of them resemble one another, each a handmade one-off. The ludicrous B-flat major is representative, flying across the plain in long cat-strides in the bass, with a frantic scramble in the upper registers, until the prey is arrested, a broken chord presaging a broken neck, before we break free once more. And yet there is a unity across all of the preludes, since they serve the same purpose. Each has a freewheeling, improvisational quality that contrasts with the succeeding fugue, where convention dictates a set structure. Accordingly, we begin each key in a slightly drunken frenzy in the prelude, before sobering up for the fugue, the one you hope your daughter marries. And each reminds us of the building blocks of music, the scales and the chords built upon them, by emphasizing one or the other quite distinctly, as in the whizzing scales of the B-flat major, or the chord patterns in C major at the very beginning of the work.

But the deepest lesson of the *The Well-Tempered Clavier* only emerged as I tried grasping the arcane details of the tuning to which the title refers. The fundamental problem was that if the keyboard was tuned by mathematically pure ratios first suggested by the Pythagoreans, then something cracked elsewhere in the system—cracked for reasons I found quite perplexing, and which reminded me of my struggles with calculus. Keyboards can thus be set up either to play perfectly in tune in one key, or slightly out of tune, in a sense, to enable playing across many keys. (Modern pianos are tempered and impure for this reason, though not in quite the same way as Bach's keyboards.) I found it surprising to learn that nearly all the music we hear is slightly out of tune by Greek standards, and even more surprising that someone like Bach, who had perfect pitch and was famous for being able to detect the slightest mistakes in tuning, would not only have accepted this but written an elaborate composition celebrating the fact.

But as I listened more intently to those forty-eight preludes and fugues, I started to see the point that Bach was ultimately making: sometimes the quest for purity is limiting; there are advantages to imperfection. In photography, the zealot humps his lenses and a tripod up the hill and waits in vain for that golden moment, when a snapshot on his phone, dangling off one leg, would be truer to the scene. Accepting impurities opened up new vistas to Bach, whose music was made flexible and nimble by tempering, which freed him to rove across the keys and connect once isolated realms. Or perhaps it is better to say that abandoning a certain mathematical perfection allows for another, more *practical* sense of perfection—one measured in terms of the greatness of the works each system makes possible. The perfect picture is one that does justice to the scene, not the one that measures up to some abstract rule. In that sense, *The Well-Tempered Clavier* is strangely self-ratifying: it demonstrates a system whose only justification can be the excellence of the demonstration itself.

Lauren and I still lived separately, even though we'd been together for many years. When she came over in the evening I would still be practicing, listening intently for the car to pull up or the key to engage so that I could stop playing and discreetly shut the lid, the way I once had *click-click-clicked* off the TV when Mother came home in the afternoon, before she could reprimand me for my indolence. Sometimes there was a slight pause when Lauren entered, before unfurling her coat, as if she were listening, and I wondered if she had heard me outside.

The problem wasn't that she didn't like music, it was the opposite. She had played the violin since she was a child, at first classical and then increasingly exotic folk traditions—bluegrass, old-time music, Swedish fiddle. But then she had developed hand problems similar to mine at just about the same time. She, too, tried getting rest and stretching and good form, she too failed to improve, and she too was advised to get a series of pointless surgeries that left her worse off than before, all of which was quite perplexing, of course. There are those old couples that seem to fade into one another, slowly coming to look the same, to catch one another's illnesses, and eventually they pass away together. But we weren't an old couple and the neurological tests suggested something more than sympathetic contagion. And yet there we were, both unable to play. At the piano, waiting for the lock to jangle, I often wondered what explained this sad synchronicity, other than our both spending too much time at keyboards and our slovenly posture, but it was impossible to say.

As agonizing as it had been for me to get a taste of Bach on the piano and then to give it up again, Lauren's loss seemed worse. To those around us our reactions seemed overdramatic, lamenting a hobby that could easily be replaced by golf or knitting, and they asked about it every few weeks the way you'd ask about indigestion, with a show of courtesy rather than a sense of horror. Musical injuries can seem trivial in the way that music itself seems ornamental to some, a wallpaper for the ears. But Father used to compare losing Mother to losing a leg or a hand, and intense memories on an anniversary to a phantom limb, the pain of a part of you injured that you wish to heal yet which no longer even exists, and I observed something similar in Lauren. Every few weeks there would be pitiful evidence of trying to regenerate the lost lizard limb, a case unzipped, some sheet music out, yet it would come to nothing and she would inexplicably cry when certain pieces came over the radio.

What is lost in such cases is elusive. It isn't just the ability to perform or to express oneself, much less a diverting pastime. For Lauren it was an organ of perception. She never shared my dislike of the major keys, and whereas for me music was more often a way of coming to terms with the severe facts of life, of all I feared or failed at, for her it was a way of registering the utmost life had to offer, to experience an unmediated joy that implied there was always hope and always more to come. After her musectomy, she seemed a little blinded to such hopes and more affected by the mundane trials of the office or family. Every now and then I tried playing for her to gauge her reaction, but for now I closed the fallboard.

I moved on to examining *The Goldberg Variations*, a set of thirty variations on an enigmatic aria at the head of the work that is repeated at the end. Long considered esoteric or even unplayable—a performance can last over an hour—Glenn Gould's 1956 recording proved the opposite, rediscovering the wit and bravura that was always there. Like *The Well-Tempered Clavier*, the *Variations* are a record of obsession, not with the cycle of key signatures, which remain quite stable, but with the theme the aria is based on and the journey back to it. Not just the work itself, but Bach's notebooks and manuscripts suggest that he spent years humming this theme and trying to work out all of its possibilities.

The *Variations* reveal a playful, mischievous side to Bach, and listening to them can be frustrating at first. What we expect to hear is a clear rendition of the tune to be varied, just as the subject of a fugue is initially played unadorned so we can get our bearings. And indeed, a charming, mysterious melody greets us at the outset, which we consequently look for in each succeeding variation, expecting to hear it slightly adjusted in rhythm or key. But while there are occasional feints or gestures back to this melody, it mostly vanishes, like Hitchcock killing off his star in the first act of *Psycho*. The real theme is hiding in the bass, and even then Bach uses a variety of tricks to hide it from us, distributing the notes across several measures, or mixing in other lines to hide the ball like a street grifter.

Why all this hoodwinking, I wondered. But as I went over the music in more detail, pecking out a few notes here or there at the piano, it seemed to me the strategy wasn't so much to trick us but to accumulate layers of meaning that waited patiently to be uncovered, while remaining entirely optional. We can move through the variations quite casually, in a daze, somnolent if we like—indeed, sleep plays an important role in the story of *The Goldberg Variations*, I later discovered—but if we awake and attend, revelations open up before us, like those fractal designs in arabesque art. For instance, most of the variations contain thirty-two measures of music, matching the thirty-two arias and variations, and then divide into ever deeper subpatterns when you zoom in. And the variations come in groups of three, carefully marked and even numbered if you know what to listen for. Each trinity follows a similar pattern. My favorite after a while was the second, which starts with a stuttering dance that builds up energy staggering leg to leg, which is then released in a torrent of notes in the following freestyle piece, which requires the pianist to cross hands back and forth and is fun to watch as well as hear. We know we've reached the end of the triad at the stately canon, a kind of ouroboros in which each voice must copy, then eat the one before it, like the round "Row, Row, Row Your Boat," while the *Goldberg* theme canters along beneath, ever in disguise.

Because of all this complexity, Bach is sometimes accused of obscurity. But just as *The Well-Tempered Clavier* suggests the advantages of imperfection, so the *Variations* seem to show that there are some advantages to obscurity, or at least to being obscure in the right *way*. The secret to listening to Bach is simply to ignore anything that seems murky until it becomes clearer as you get sucked in further and further. There are shadows at the bottom of the pond, but we're welcome to paddle along the surface. In this, Bach is quite unlike James Joyce or avant-garde music, which is often impenetrable from the outset (and thus obscure in the wrong way), however rewarding after some exertion, and different again from Mozart or Hemingway, who can challenge us after a fashion, but rarely seem esoteric.

As I approached the end and arrived back at the aria, I noted that we seemed to have moved through another great circle, calling to mind the movement through the cycle of keys in *The Well-Tempered Clavier*. In one sense, of course, this was perfectly familiar; arriving back where we come from is satisfying, and nowhere more so than in music. But Bach was beginning to seem unusually fixated on cycles. And in the *Variations* we aren't just revolving endlessly—with more time, you felt there could have been another three or four books of *The Well-Tempered Clavier*—but rather, we seem to be returning *home*. Later, when I read some Bach biographies, this sense of Bach's "home" became a bit more concrete, but for now, I could hear it in the return to the aria, whose repetition wasn't in the least a foregone conclusion.

Bach's fixation reminded me of Homer and *The Odyssey*, whose stories are of the homecomings—the *nostoi*—of the heroes of the Trojan war, and whose central question runs, "So, you are home again at long last, but could you possibly be the same as you were before?" They are stories not just of return but of transformation and of revised perception. More mundanely, the *Variations* called to mind returning to the United States after living in Germany as a child (perhaps Bach had been in the air in our little village) and the strange experience of seeing pop culture and junk food in a new light. (In the U.S., people thought you were odd if you hadn't watched *Brady Bunch* reruns, and even odder if you ate dark bread, while in Germany every hamlet had an opera but no one understood sitcoms.) At the end of the *Variations*, having heard the sirens singing each to each and spoken with the dead, you realize that you thought you knew what the aria was about—that pretty tune in the soprano—but that it was something else entirely, that the variations formed a random hodgepodge when they were strictly grouped in threes, and that somehow this vast variety of music from the last hour was all implicit in the simple line you heard (or didn't quite hear) at the outset, and finally that through the variations—the German term literally means "changes"—Bach has made you a little more his student and a student of counterpoint.

After a while, I couldn't bear the childish things I was practicing, and I decided to look at what Bach himself thought I should play. This came in the form of Anna Magdalena's music book—a collection of mostly easy pieces Bach wrote for his second wife, perhaps when she was learning, or when she was helping the kids to learn. To my delight, these weren't really any harder than the rubbish I'd been working on. At first, I continued studying with my adult beginner's book alongside, but eventually I ditched it altogether. In fact, in the course of teaching his wife, his children, his students, and essentially all of humanity, Bach had created a sequence of works whose difficulty level was perfectly graded from neophyte all the way to virtually unplayable material for experts.

As a student, I couldn't believe my good fortune that there should exist this smoothly graded path. With a few exceptions, there was no point to exercises or special-purpose learning materials at all. Once you could identify the piano in your room, you could start learning Bach. I pledged, somewhat unrealistically, not to learn anything else, and to climb this gentle slope through Anna's music book, up into the two-part inventions, and then the easier pieces from *The Well-Tempered Clavier*, then the harder ones, culminating on a distant peak in *The Art of Fugue*, a peak I could not even see from my supine position at the foot of the mountain.

Except for Christopher, my various musical acquaintances disapproved of this plan, insisting that without a host of technical exercises I would never amount to any-thing. (Christopher, on the other hand, took the view that tempo was the only thing that mattered, and that as long as I played slowly enough it didn't matter what I started with.) But the trouble was that my hands only permitted me a very limited amount of practice time, and I was desperate that that time should go to something rewarding. And while I was prepared to admit that at some point I might need to look into those exercises, for the moment I couldn't resist working on, first, the Minuet in G Major from the music book, and its companion in G minor. These seemed to me of the utmost perfection, and the fugues I so loved were more complex, but not better.

For a long time I wondered how Bach could have wasted such melodies on a mere notebook. I was amazed to discover that in fact these particular pieces seem not to have been Bach's creation at all, but some obscure contem-porary's, included in the book for their pedagogical value. They were thus merely indications of his perfect taste, and perhaps that was why those melodies weren't put to a more elevated use. But ultimately there must have been some deeper explanation for this "waste," since a great many of the pedagogical pieces Bach wrote contained gemlike materials that a 19th-century composer would have hoarded for some special occasion, like a grandmaster saving chess novelties for the big match.

The real explanation of all this seeming waste was perhaps twofold. First, Bach's talent had an overflowing, unbounded quality that didn't require saving up for great occasions; he simply sat down to write, and good ideas poured out, sometimes better and sometimes better still. Second, I gradually realized how much humility was evident in the music I was studying. Here was the greatest composer of all time, and he was spending hours, countless hours, in creating fancy editions of his teaching manuals there was no reason to suspect anyone else would ever see. And it wasn't just Anna's music book: a large amount of the non-liturgical music Bach composed was either directly pedagogical, or makes every impression of being intended ultimately to help with technique. There is no sense that such work is beneath him, that he is a grand composer with better things to do, or that these are fake etudes, practice-pieces in name only that are destined for the concert hall.

I now imagined myself joining the Bach family, perhaps with Anna or little Wilhelm alongside at the keyboard, playing music composed or carefully curated by the old man himself. I wasn't learning alone; I was part of the family, and my mistakes weren't any worse, perhaps, than those of the other children.

If we change out the lens of counterpoint for a moment, we can also see Bach's music as a compendium of international styles. If we lost all of the music by Baroque composers from France, Italy, and northern Europe, we could reconstruct a great deal of it simply by working backward from Bach, though we would arrive at a greatly inflated estimate of its quality. One could similarly reconstruct the national character of these peoples from their music. Schoolmarms would scold the results as impolitic and stereotyped (even as they drove off in their German cars to eat in Italian restaurants), but we would recognize their essential truth.

The French composers were pompous and arrogant, still celebrating Louis XIV, the Sun King, when Bach was thirty. The pastry puff in D major in *The Well-Tempered Clavier*, with its long dotted notes, takes a French overture for its inspiration, as does the sixteenth *Goldberg* variation at the halfway mark. The regal dotted notes command reverence as the king enters—a king who dances, but a king all the same. The conductor is Jean-Baptiste Lully; he directs the royal orchestra with an enormous staff he thrusts so vigorously that one day he stabs himself in the foot, which he refuses to amputate because then he could no longer dance à la mode, and so he dies from his gangrenous wound. Bach, despite this inauspicious example, ambles after Lully and the French, not always keeping up, a little the Hephaestus, always with a bit of a limp, perhaps in honor of Lully's injury. The stylish French dance with whimsy and abandon; Lully and his successor Couperin twist and turn, inserting wild flourishes and fantastical ornamentation—trills and grace notes to decorate the pastry without contributing to its structure, which immediately collapses when you take a hard bite. In Bach, all of the characteristic dances of the French are reproduced with a slightly labored fidelity to the time signatures and flavors of the original, albeit with infinitely greater depth of counterpoint, and less both of Gallic pomp and whimsy. (By contrast, Handel's *Messiah* reproduces the French overture style almost slavishly.) These dances make up the substance of Bach's suites, like *The French Suites* or *The English Suites*, or his keyboard partitas, giving them a distinctly cosmopolitan feel.

Meanwhile, the Italians with their tradition of opera and opulence perfected a melismatic style, which meant spinning out each syllable into several petticoated notes. Their instrumental music, accordingly, was cantabile, singsong, with smooth, fluid lines, derived from vocal practice, the very opposite of the stiff counterpoint up north. To create drama, the Italians often alternated between the full orchestra and solo instruments, passing themes and variations on them back and forth in a technique we recognize from Vivaldi's *Four Seasons*. Yet in his syncretic fervor, Bach sought to assimilate even this music. His orchestral pieces, like the disastrously baroque-sounding *Brandenburg Concertos,* follow the alternating pattern, and the far superior passions, especially the *St Matthew*, are essentially Italian operas adapted for the church. Even the keyboard music makes the unlikely leap to melisma here and there, as in the second movement of *The Italian Concerto*, or the first movement of the keyboard Partita in C Minor.

But of course the most characteristic style in Bach is the northern Protestant approach. One might say that all the other traditions are ultimately filtered through and expressed in this dialect—French, Italian, early Renaissance, operatic, dance music, all repeated with a light accent. Listening to a simple fugue like my beloved C minor, by contrast, sounds like someone speaking in their native tongue, without accommodation or compromise. Bach cannot quite bring himself to turn his soundly structured masterpieces into ornamented éclairs, or to leave out contrapuntal texture to facilitate singsong. There is a tension, in other words, between Bach the universalist, who absorbs and synthesizes every instrument, key signature, form, and nationality, supplementing each with his own native genius, and Bach the particularist, the Lutheran born in Eisenach, who grew up listening to the organ and eating beets and cabbages, who hummed lustily, "Ich bin so lang nicht bei dir gewest" walking to school.

Working through Anna Magdalena's notebook, I considered how I had arrived at this odd position, of reverse-adopting Papa Bach in lieu of a teacher. The suffering of our past selves rarely moves us in the present, and I lamented that my parents hadn't forced me to take years of painful music lessons so that I could have gotten the routine work out of the way long ago. Now, each moment was precious, whereas back then the opportunity cost had been practically nothing, childhood consisting mostly of rolling around in dirt.

I had been raised, like most Americans, as a semiliterate peasant, directed mainly toward athletics and the practical knowledge required to make money. Doing well in school was important, but that just meant stumbling through a series of farcical rituals—the egg drop, the science project (which toilet paper absorbs best?), *The Catcher in the Rye*, and other patriotic lightweights. Instead of learning Bach, I wandered through soccer fields picking at dandelions as the ball sailed over my head; I was flung about on the judo mat; I lost myself in the ecstasy of the ping-pong smash. My parents exhibited astonishing perseverance in supporting all of these tortures, faithfully attending each game I helped lose, ceaselessly proposing new activities to replace the old ones—almost anything as long as it didn't involve music.

I could hardly blame them. My parents, each in their own way, faced brutal conditions I would never know, involving (somehow!) the Nazis as well as the Soviets, jungle warfare, and selling pots and pans door to door, giving them little sympathy for the delicate arts. The only music my father responded to was the more aggressive species of marching band, the kind you imagined preceding a column of tanks, and while my mother painted a little, she couldn't carry a tune. (If anything, it was my brother's heavy metal tapes that prepared the way, with its emphasis on recurring riffs and virtuosic guitar solos.) As a result, our record collection was a harrowing witness to poor taste, the musical equivalent of Wonder Bread and Twinkies, and a musical education wasn't in the cards.

Even so, I owed Mother my first acquaintance with Bach, looking through these records in high school and stumbling on Glenn Gould's recording of *The Art of Fugue* wedged between Kenny Rogers and ABBA, which was like finding a Bugatti in your garage one day. How in the world had it gotten there? She died before I thought to ask. This discovery seemed to me either incredibly lucky or else it revealed some hidden destiny at work. It was comforting to think that all those egg drops and all that rolling around in dirt hadn't made much of a difference: Bach and the piano were always out there waiting—it was just a question of time.

There were, of course, certain disadvantages to starting late and learning from the dead. I lacked the sense of terror to motivate me; there was no one to shame me when I put on a poor performance. I messaged Christopher frequently for advice, but sometimes it was hard to explain what was going on. On the other hand, Papa Bach had had to teach himself in many respects, and so I felt I was imitating him in this, as well. Many keyboard players in his time didn't even use their thumbs, and so Bach taught himself even the rudiments of fingering and hand positioning. And, on a more philosophical level, I was spared not just the emotional terrorism present in most teaching relationships—you can't obtain the motivational benefits of terror without the corresponding drawbacks—but some of the indignities that students face, like the way that students start out disappointing their teachers but end up disappointed *in* them, just as children end up disappointed in their parents. (Which, I sometimes wondered, was worse? The inability to meet your guru's expectations or the melancholy insight that your guru is flecked and flawed and that you are ultimately on your own?)

Reflecting on Bach's music, on what it said about counterpoint and why it moved me so deeply, I returned in the end to *The Art of Fugue*. Of course, there were many other pieces worth belaboring. I was especially fascinated by the works for solo instruments, since they seem to pose an insurmountable problem for the contrapuntalist: How can you interweave multiple voices when you have only the one instrument at your disposal? Counterpoint counter to *what*? The solution could be found in pieces like the monumental Chaconne in D Minor for solo violin, a fifteen-minute giant completely out of proportion with the other movements that it follows—a conclusion of searing intensity that melts away rather than consolidating what came before. Somehow Bach manages to *imply* counterpoint even here, and a trained-up listener slowly starts to hear the other lines fading in against the darkness, like writing on the bathroom mirror. Dueling high and low voices suggest a dialogue rather than monologue; peaks and troughs in a wavelike phrase hint at conversation. Often this music is far from idiomatic to the violin. It's a solo instrument, we might protest—why can't Bach just focus on the pure, solitary line? No one should have to sing alone, he seems to say.

Still, it is *The Art of Fugue* that feels like the summit. Perhaps that is because it is one of his last and unfinished works—there is a sense in which he died writing it—and because the music and title suggest that he was trying to sum up all that he had learned about fugues. It comes down to us both incomplete and in fragments, with arguments continuing to this day about exactly what the intended structure and order was, and whether some of the more celebrated pieces were meant to be a part of it at all. The conceit is to produce a large-scale work based on a single, quite simple theme, using the various fugues and canons that follow to introduce successively more complex ideas about that theme, for instance by flipping it on its head in inversion, or augmenting the note values so that it sounds slower, in a series of dizzying transformations. And at the very end, the original theme returns and is triumphantly combined with all that has come before, like the return to the aria in *The Goldberg Variations*. But in this case, the score breaks off, just at the point where Bach introduces a theme spelling out his name, *B-A-C-H*. (In German music theory, *B* indicates B-flat and *H* indicates a plain B-natural.)

The Art of Fugue has a mesmerizing purity. There is no attempt at accommodating fashion or taste, the opera or dance suites, or trivial facts about human anatomy and what it is physically possible to play. Its style was considered reactionary even at the time, as the streamlined forms we associate with Haydn or Mozart were starting to emerge. Counterpoint, at least in the dense manner of Bach, was going out of style, making this more a temple to a dying faith than a celebration of it. There isn't even an indication of which instrument the piece was meant for, but that, too, has its meaning. When you write a mathematical proof it doesn't matter what color ink you use. The piece may be played on virtually any instrument (with the exception, obviously, of the bloody harpsichord), or in ensemble, or on the organ as Glenn Gould did on my Mother's recording.

Sometimes all this technical perfection strikes people as cold or austere. But there is plenty of pathos and humanity to be found in *The Art of Fugue* as in the rest of Bach; sometimes it just comes in subtler forms than we're accustomed to. Bach's perfections are more like the faint smile in a Vermeer or the quality of light through his windows than the technicolor of Michelangelo. A passing tone, a clashing interval may be all there is to express infinite sadness and loss. If we're new to this, we may be surprised when the point isn't circled with a big red pen, marked fortissimo in the score lest we miss the big moment, but once we are accustomed to the smaller scale, it's hard to go back, and listening to Beethoven's codas feels like someone sneezing in your face. The opening piece, for example, builds to a climax through a series of violent upward leaps to plateaus that themselves form a descending line, all across a tense pedal note in the bass. Then come a series of abrupt rests, prompting us to wonder if we really just might leave everything unresolved, leave the hero dead at the end of the story, only for the music to sputter back to life at the last instant and give us our resolution, but one we're suspicious of now, prepared to second-guess. And in the end our suspicions prove well-founded when the last piece is supposed to return us home (Ilium sacked, enemies desecrated), but perhaps we've done too much to deserve a tranquil homecoming, and *The Art of Fugue* ends unfinished in a hideous wreck.

Why, then, Bach in particular? All that stuff about counterpoint and realizing music's deepest possibilities was true, and the more you listened to *The Well-Tempered Clavier*, *The Goldberg Variations*, or *The Art of Fugue*, the more deeply you felt it. There is nothing wrong with Vivaldi's simple lines (or with pop, for that matter), any more than there is with Hemingway's clipped sentences, but it's hard to feel any of these is pushing the language to its limits, doing things "unattempted yet in prose or rhyme," as Milton puts it. The brilliance of Bach's native tradition was to unite melody and harmony, the vertical and horizontal, in a way that no other tradition has ever really tried or shows any signs of trying again. But now I started to feel that there was something deeper still in the carousel of departures and homecomings, of absurd, distempered voyages into anarchy (midway through *The Art of Fugue* one starts thinking of Werner Herzog movies about madmen lost in the jungle, or of Magellan speared on the shores of Mactan) that nevertheless strain back always for a home that is either lost or so irrevocably altered as to feel more like a point of departure for another cycle than genuine rest.

I found that as the flecks of gray in my hair broke into solid streaks, often what I thought I felt about the work of an artist was instead something about their character that the work revealed, and perhaps this was true of Bach as well. I liked the novels of Henry James because, beneath the thicket of prose and infinitely refined observations, he was a naïve American unafraid of moral judgment, of bourgeois blame, and I didn't like Flaubert or James Joyce because they didn't pass judgment at all—they understood all and forgave all even when they shouldn't have understood a thing. In Bach, it was a bizarre combination of humility and arrogance I detected and which fascinated me, and made me wish I knew more about him. On the one hand, his mature music is devoid of flashy gestures or histrionics; he never puts on airs. He eschews the flowery, ornamental style the French were fond of in his time, and also the huffing and puffing of a Beethoven or Mahler.

He cheerfully dedicates his best ideas to beginner's pieces for his wife and kids. To the extent that *The Goldberg Variations* and *The Art of Fugue* strike us as epics—and they should—they do so not because of any bombast but because of how far they carry us before depositing us again on familiar shores. On the other hand, Bach is hardly lacking in confidence or ambition. On the contrary, anyone announcing that he was going to compose not one but two cycles of preludes and fugues in every key to demonstrate music's deepest possibilities would sound arrogant if not crazy, and yet that is what Bach in effect does. For reasons I found hard to articulate, this combination of humility and supreme competence, verging on arrogance, moved me intensely, perhaps because it is so rare. Those who have been humbled tend to be unambitious, while those with talent lack the humility to restrain themselves from hubris and vulgarity. The music of Bach dares things unattempted yet, but never feels the need to tell us so.

3

The Struggle

After a year or so, I was ready to try Bach's two-part inventions, written for students just like me. This seemed a momentous step, since the music was now evenly distributed between the left and the right hand, and began to sound like art, not just exercises. And because they were written for people destined to be composers—his children and other students—they also gave insight into composition and how Bach went about constructing a piece.

My initial plan was to skip all of the major key numbers, but that proved impossible, despite myself, once I stumbled through the opening bars of the first invention in C major. The music was absurdly simple: just a few notes from the C major scale up and down, then a leap and a trill—an ornament consisting of the rapid alternation between two notes. It was all so logical: figure out what key you are in, noodle around in the scale until you find something reasonably catchy, modulate to related keys now and then according to some straightforward rules, and return home.

But what about counterpoint? For the most part, the earlier exercises I had practiced were written for a single voice, with occasional accompaniment in the other hand. But now there were two living, equal lines, one for each hand, with their own identity, mind, and will. Where did the other voice come from? The answer, I could now see, derived from the concept of imitation. For when the right hand was finished stating its homely theme, the left hand simply repeated it, harmonizing with the new material in the right hand, and similarly for a great deal of the piece; the two voices took turns as leader and follower, handing off material like a baton among relay runners, now cooperating, now teasing and taunting each other, before settling the rivalry in the last measure.

From one point of view, this imitative counterpoint was a sly, lazy trick: for the most part, it meant the composer only had to think up one set of musical ideas instead of two. But this was the wrong way of looking at things: figuring out how to make sure that everything harmonized by *itself* was no mean feat, since it meant the composer wasn't free to adjust his melody for the sake of harmonizing—one of those melodies was already fixed by what the leader had sung. The snake had to be ready to eat its tail. And in any case, as I began learning the piece, I found myself delighting in the interplay between the voices, by the sense of chase and drama, like two dogs tussling over the same bone. Since my sight-reading skills were poor, it was hard to translate all this into my hands, but I found that it helped to guess a bit where the music was going, checking the page every so often to be sure, though Bach seemed to notice this ploy, and threw in some nasty jumps to keep you honest.

The trill in this piece introduced me to the first technical skill that I found physically impossible. It was maddening: since a trill is just an ornament, akin to a grace note, it was in a sense trivial, yet crucial to the feel of the music, to adding a sense of polish and sheen to a surface otherwise too dull, like the flashes of light in the paintings of Rembrandt or Whistler. And yet my fingers simply would not play these rapid notes, at least not with the casual flourish they required. This may not seem surprising since I was a rank beginner, and many such inabilities were to follow, but it perplexed me nevertheless: my brain instructed my fingers what to do, there was no question of strength or muscle power, and yet my fingers simply wouldn't obey. Mental causation failed me. I frowned sternly at middle and index fingers, issued dire imprecations, but they maintained their sluggish, vermicular form, and produced not so much a trill as a *traaaalch.* I spent twenty minutes playing trill after trill to improve, but after a while there was a burning sensation in my forearms that frightened me, and I resigned myself to learning the rest of the music while practicing this technical problem on the side.

Trill aside, after a few more weeks I felt immensely proud of all the progress I'd made on my invention. By then I had memorized the music and could play nearly the whole piece with my eyes closed. It was time to formalize my triumph by making a recording and surprising Christopher with it. I found this a little difficult because setting up the phone to record made me self-conscious, as if someone else were in the room, and I avoided playing in front of others at all costs, but after a few practice runs I captured what I took to be a rather impressive version. I played smoothly from start to finish at a rapid clip, made my little jumps, and when the fast section came, my fingers flew across the keyboard toward a conclusion that was at least trill-*like.* I pumped my fist in the air, trimmed the video, and without watching it much, messaged Christopher.

At first he didn't reply, and I was annoyed that he didn't seem interested in my important achievement. Then I began to worry. Was it possible I had made some sort of mistake? Perhaps I had missed an accidental somewhere and played a false note? I pulled up the video to study it more closely, and I couldn't believe it: somehow my rapid, elegant playing hadn't been captured by the camera at all. Instead, I saw my fingers stumbling across the keyboard like a drunken octopus. The tempo was absurdly slow; the trills were awkward and strained; it barely sounded like music at all. But I quickly learned that this assessment was still much too generous. For when Christopher wrote back later in the day, his tone was equal parts pity, alarm, and professional disdain. I shouldn't be too hard on myself—many students struggled with the concept of rhythm. Did I not own a metronome? Had I figured out how to use it? Still, he said, I should avoid suggesting three different tempos in the first two measures.

I was angry, and went back to the video one more time to confirm this was nonsense. Of course I had a metronome, of course I practiced with it—at least now and then, just as I flossed regularly if the dentist asked. But now it was as if I heard myself for the first time, really heard myself as others did, and it was horrifying, the way hearing our own alien-sounding voice on a recording can be, or the way overhearing our friends talking about us can jolt us to our core. Christopher's detached observations had dissolved the layers of ego muffling my ears. Sure enough: I wasn't playing a single tempo, not even in the first bar. It was horribly uneven. When I was playing passages I found easy I sped up, and when I hit parts that were more difficult, or that required me to play with my weaker fingers, I either slowed down, or stretched out measures, or altered the force with which I depressed the keys, leading again to unevenness. The fact of the matter was that despite knowing the music, I was utterly incapable of playing it correctly.

At that point I couldn't be angry with Christopher any longer—it wasn't his fault that I had sent him this trash. Of course, if I had been playing with a teacher week by week, I would have been spared this sudden epiphany, but on the other hand getting the jolt all at once had more of an effect than a trickle of reproach. As it was, I could hardly forget that pride dulls the senses. Playing the piano now became a spiritual exercise, practically Ignatian in its rigors—not that it was contemplative, but it meant continually failing (if you weren't failing, you were wasting your time) and trying to admit these failures and to correct them. Playing the piano meant seeing yourself for what you really were, and I began to appreciate that learning an instrument begins with self-revelation and then proceeds either to self-contempt or else to mediocrity.

After this catastrophe, I no longer trusted myself. Things might sound all right to me, but who could say? A certain paranoia set in, the skepticism of Descartes, who pointed out that the people around us could all be automata for all we know, since what we really see are hats and overcoats, and the rest is dogma or inference. Sometimes this produced a sense of panic, like when Mother had died, and suddenly the possibility of death, which I had never taken too seriously, filled the entire field of view, and I couldn't understand why *I* was thought strange for being unable to sleep or eat. In response, I took to recording myself frequently, and after a while I found that the mere threat of pressing "record" was enough for me to own up.

I also kept the metronome running more or less permanently, *tock-tock-tock*. It was the sound of naked truth, the voice of God, though it was exhausting to fight against this objective pattern. I would come to one of those difficult passages and persuade myself that time itself had slowed down for a while so that I could get in all the notes, and yet the metronome disagreed. After one of these conflicts I would wonder whether the metronome wasn't perhaps defective; it seemed to skip ahead impishly on certain beats, so that I was always slightly off. On other occasions, I developed wild suspicions that the metronome was plotting against me, or that it was a competitor I was racing against, whom I could conquer by playing faster than the beat.

Meanwhile, I kept working on that trill, and was amazed at how stubborn my hands remained. My conscious self would issue instructions through the pineal gland that were relayed by strings down through my limbs and into my fingers, which promptly froze up. I wished I could have been one of those mannequin musicians they built in the 18th century, not this concatenation of members that seemed so outmatched by the enemy, *tock-tock-tock*. And these failures seemed all the more puzzling once I found that passages that had seemed all but impossible practicing them the night before were playable the next day, as if a database on a server somewhere ran a batch of scripts overnight, and I had no choice but to wait for the update. The gap between our aspirations and our abilities alienates us from whatever stands in the way, even, at the limit, ourselves. And yet, it was all so absurd, when I thought about it—the very meaning of my life seemed to depend on whether I could fling my fingers down just so, as if someone were to declare his life hinged on whether he could wiggle his ears a certain way or touch his nose with his tongue; it had all the vast consequence of nuclear war, but concentrated into something so small, so trivial-seeming.

The problem in ethics is to be neither too human nor inhuman, but just human enough, and the same in music. The radicals get this all wrong and declare humanity a mistake, and send millions to their deaths in search of the ideal, while the other party shrugs at our crooked timber and won't even straighten a plank. The problem of the piano is to become a part of the machine while retaining the sludge of organism, a hybrid that aspires to grow, but never beyond its roots.

There are strange reversals in what we take to be our avocations and side-projects, and what we count as the real thing. Acquaintances become friends or lovers and weekend distractions become our income. Slowly, playing Bach came to seem like what really mattered, and it bothered me more and more to be called away to the office, where I sat all day and dreamt of those cycles and homecomings.

The fact that I worked as a teacher while struggling so ineffectually at the piano made this daily distraction all the more peculiar. And in truth, while teaching people things they actually want to learn is a great delight (Shivani had just submitted an ingenious paper on tragedy that emerged almost visibly from an exchange in class), teaching is in reality rarely so straightforward. I found myself wondering whether part of why I was so resistant to becoming a piano student was that I felt ambivalent about being a teacher. To be a student is to be invigilated, hectored, examined, bored, reprimanded, bullied, terrorized, dictated, lied to, and neglected—all true; but to be a teacher is to perform in front of hundreds of kids who regard you as an incompetent entertainer, who often groan at the slightest attempt to foster talent or skill, and then to be judged by a series of sham evaluations written by anonymous teenagers on the Internet.

The semester begins with a lecture hall filled with hundreds of hopeful, shining faces, but then there are five percent fewer each week; they begin to sink into their gadgets; and you must choose between seeming friendly and hip, and chastising students like a tedious scold, when all you ever wanted was to read some books and talk about them for a living. The lecture hall is enormous and dehumanizing; learning people's names is out of the question, and therefore you must maintain a generalized half-smile when wandering the campus just in case you run into someone who greets you, to which you can only reply with a vague but enthusiastic nod. And when you do finally mentor face-to-face, you must gauge carefully their capacity to withstand censure and humiliation, which are required for progress, and yet most students are unwilling to tolerate either, and if they do, you feel terrible observing the shame settle in when you offer honest feedback, and you vacillate between hoping they will be *un*shameable and thus impervious to criticism as well as improvement, or else ductile and teachable, which means they're crushed when you point out the inevitable flaws in their work. Optimists think there's an easy way out with joyful, positive reinforcement, but what is the joyful way of telling someone that they've failed?

Far worse, being a teacher generally means joining a vast bureaucracy. In any classroom there's the occasional moment of getting through, of shattering the general indifference, but there's no escape from the squadrons of administrators promoting the latest fads, as if the last five thousand years of human education did not exist or had failed somehow to educate anyone. Mandatory training seminars, dean's advisory meetings, teaching excellence programs—these and many other horrors separated me from my piano. I found refuge in keeping ever more silent at these meetings, both in order not to prolong them, and to reflect on the music I was working on and what I would practice when I got back. Christopher had once quipped that German silence is structural, while French silence is merely ornamental (riffing, he claimed, on Glenn Gould), and I found I could keep up my musical studies quite effectively by practicing this structural silence, the music of the mind, as it were, while the vice assistant dean for Academic Affairs droned on about the latest plan for the Teaching Transformation Center.

I arrived at the Invention in F Major worn out from these struggles. I had thought that I would be able to play each piece as I went along nearly perfectly, and getting better would simply mean playing more complex music. But if anything it was the opposite: there wasn't anything particularly preventing me from playing complicated music on the spot, only I would play it badly, just as I played the simple music I was working on badly. Getting better didn't so much mean handling more complicated material, though it did, as learning to play anything at all with grace and precision.

The C major had been a simple lesson in scales, but the F major added arpeggios—chords in which the notes are played sequentially instead of being struck all at once—and an arsenal of technical tricks. Playing it produced an exhilaration I had never thought possible and had never experienced before, one that almost redeemed the major keys, and from then on, whenever there was darkness and gloom, whenever I was tempted to despair of learning the instrument, I returned to this invention, which isn't merely cheerful or happy, but sheer condensed *joy*. It begins by outlining the fundamental chord, F major, but does so by nervously exploring the hill around its burrow, starting on F, darting up to A, then back home to F, up a little higher to C, back down to F, then a daring leap an octave higher, only to roll back down by lazy, undulating steps, while the left hand begins the chase with its own tiptoe maneuver. They finally meet and harmonize in a kind of glockenspiel maneuver.

The sense of surprise and of exhilaration continued all the while learning the piece, since you often cannot understand what is happening in a passage until you play it fluidly enough to see what the composer intended, or to hear the musical rhymes, in which one passage seems to call for a response, or see why an ugly-sounding moment makes sense in context. At times if I listened just right, I could hear the music speaking some natural language, as if I just needed to study a little more German or Polish or Latin, and I would understand what it was saying, if only "Practice harder!" Each tiptoe up the hill and roll back down, each chase, catch, and release, each antiphon was an ode to joy in miniature, one that didn't rely on bombast or shock, classically proportioned and perfect, a world in a measure of music, infinity under the palms of my hands. It was impossible not to sing while playing these notes, and I suddenly understood why Glenn Gould hummed over his recordings, including of this piece.

But eventually the euphoria wore away, and I was left with the mundane problem of actually playing these notes. I hadn't really gotten much better. Learning the music was trivial, but playing it correctly was not. I constantly misjudged how difficult various sections would turn out to be. Frequently my initial approach would work for a while, but as I got closer to full tempo I would realize that I had been cheating in some way, and that to make progress I would need to start over using a new fingering or pattern of emphasis. Alternatively, I would reach what had seemed a point of proficiency, only to realize that from my new, better-informed vantage point my playing was still clumsy, my two hands not really together, my tempo slightly off. And then I would periodically forget the notes themselves and have to learn them over again, as my hands seemed confused by the multiple similar but different passages. Losing my muscle memory like this would cost me hours or days as I went back to the score which I still could not sight-read easily. Learning the piano at this stage was thus full of false peaks that I would triumphantly surmount, only to realize that I was on a minor foothill that blocked the view of the real mountaintop, which stood miles away in the clouds.

Ever since Christopher had opened my ears I couldn't bear to send him more recordings of my performances. Instead, I sent him brief fragments, problem cases, seeking advice, to which his replies were tireless and full of insight. When we identified my complete lack of rhythm as a problem, for instance, he urged that falling off an established tempo was better than speeding up, as falling behind the leader is better than ramming into him; that I should avoid an overreliance on the metronome and rather strive to find the living pulse in the music; and that rhythm was ultimately more important than pitch, that it was a greater sin to lose the pulse than play a wrong note—as if they'd notice!—to keep rhythm at all costs, even at the expense of cacophony, to maintain airspeed to avoid a stall, even if it meant flying in the wrong direction. But for each trenchant email with a marked up score and Roman numeral analysis, there were puzzling suggestions as well—to imitate Gould's technique of tapping on the fingers as they lay upon the keys, which was supposed to trick the mind into seeing how little force was necessary to play them, or to think of the piano as playing me instead of vice versa, or to let gravity push down the keys on my behalf. Then, amid these koans, he would completely transform my playing with a throwaway remark about how to finger some difficult passage.

More important than the particulars, though, was the gradual absorption of Christopher into my superego, whereby the steady trickle of texts and emails massed into a musical conscience that began speaking to me even when I hadn't heard from him for weeks. I would lapse from form, and a phantom tingle would agitate my thigh even though my phone was in the other room, as if Christopher were telepathically buzzing me to signal his disapproval. Remorse would set in, the backbite of guilt, and I would mend my ways. And really, what else does a student need? I knew as a teacher how little of what I conveyed was anything the students couldn't come to on their own. They wrote poorly—they oppressed me with mangled syntax, they broke my heart with malapropisms—but not because they were ignorant; their spoken English was fine. What they mostly needed was inspiration, a little advice, standards for success, and seeds of a superego. I found myself prizing apart this cluster that was normally found together in a music teacher. The music was its own inspiration for me, and the Internet contained plenty of advice on particular pieces, and now Christopher had become my Jiminy Cricket.

But conscience has its drawbacks. The grownup suffers enormously traversing the initial stages sensitive to his musical faults, none of which register as an obtuse child. A four-year-old is perfectly happy plunking away inaccurately for years, and if his parents are indulgent he will pride himself on his progress instead of reflecting on his musical, intellectual, and spiritual inadequacies. By contrast, the adult learner is liable to perceive all too keenly how poor his playing is for many years without being able to do much to correct it. On the other hand, I was skeptical that children possessed the additional advantage of learning more quickly because of their supposed spongelike brains. We adults seem dull and inflexible once we reach a certain age, drawing on experience rather than genius, mostly just to prop things up and coast along, while children seem to learn anything. But is this because adults find it harder to learn such things as music or have we simply become lazy and unmotivated? How many middle-agers actually *try* to learn an instrument or master Ancient Greek; how many of us have our enthusiasms stamped out in the cubicle or quashed taking the kids to practice, depriving us of the energy for projects our minds remain quite fit for, telling ourselves we needn't regret this indolence because we lack the amazing minds of our children, who cannot count to ten?

Christopher himself was not at all convinced by my theory of the superego, and continued to urge various esoteric or labor-intensive techniques. I was to master all of Dohnányi's exercises before playing any of the inventions; I was to perfect every piece I learned at a creeping adagio before proceeding any faster; I was to play special exercises he recorded for me in every key before trying to play anything I actually enjoyed. I tried some of these exercises, but soon discovered that all forms of practice were interchangeable, like methods of psychotherapy or positions in sex, that all did the same good, since sectarian theories in these matters were generally nonsense, and what mattered was just doing *something*. This blasé attitude drove Christopher mad, but I became more and more convinced it was correct: what mattered were just the hours, spending those endless hours banging away, and short of practicing with your toes instead of your fingers it really didn't matter how you spent that time, as pilots measure flight time to assess experience, and pay no mind which bits of land they've flown over.

In any case, there was a certain hypocrisy in Christopher's advice, though this reflected the general hypocrisy of all teachers. He insisted that I should learn to play each piece perfectly, independent of tempo, at one beat per minute if necessary, and only then gradually practice at a faster pace. Anything else—jumping in at a challenging but not impossible tempo, and playing slightly unevenly as a result—elicited from him the disdain of a theological purist confronted with sin. When I mentioned that I was working on an invention he would ask me my tempo, and then sigh at my folly if I confessed that I was already cantering without having utterly mastered trotting. It reminded me of when I had told Mother I no longer believed in God, and she expressed a revilement that my naïve faith in love hadn't prepared me for. And yet, for all his admonitions, I couldn't help recall how Christopher had started playing Mozart's symphonies in transcription within the first six months of learning the piano, which I now realized was completely impossible without destroying one's form and wrecking one's body. I recognized this hypocrisy within myself, too, when I barked at my own students for not looking up every single word they didn't know, exasperated they should read sentences without comprehending their full meanings, or attempt *The Odyssey* before reading *The Iliad*, baffling me with their slovenly habits, that nevertheless didn't prevent them from making great progress over the years—to my considerable annoyance. (There is nothing more irritating than intrepid youth disproving the maxims of shriveled age.)

There was, I found, an unbridgeable gap between student and teacher. Christopher told me I needed to start thinking about Mozart and Beethoven to improve my technique; I bitterly pointed out that he had dropped out of music school after a brutal oral exam and now smoked fish for a living (which I regretted when my head stopped spinning the next morning); he sulked over the piano and played a mock-imitation of my invention in five different tempos. I gazed enviously on his spindly fingers, which resembled the face-hugging xenomorph in *Alien*, and sometimes prompted impossible performance suggestions. Not everyone was 6' 5" and lanky, as he was. Teachers look back over their hard-won experience eager to force their students onto paths that only make sense from the finish line, from which those routes look straight and sure, while students hack their way through the undergrowth, up one hill and down another, unsure of their progress and moved more by what seems expedient at the moment than grand strategy. Bach, though, the ultimate teacher, was silent as a sphinx: he left a series of milestones to meet, without saying anything about how to meet them. I kept to my theory of the superego and the hours, and hacked and clawed my way through another invention, as Christopher sadly shook his head.

The inventions I was working on were all in two voices, running from C major through B minor. These, I assumed, would all be of comparable difficulty, each of them easier than anything in three voices. Christopher warned me that this way of thinking was superficial, but I ignored him on the theory—another theory—that anything in two parts that could be split up neatly between left and right hands must be simpler than music for three voices split between the two, which seemed incomprehensible to me. Thus, I came to the Invention in B Minor.

Before, trills had featured only occasionally for emphasis. Now they appeared in the main theme, which was shuttled around both hands and various fingers. And yet the trill needed to sound exactly the same each time, even though some fingers are naturally stronger than others, and some positions more awkward than others. Achieving this consistency seemed both necessary and impossible. I took as my inspiration the machine gun riff in Metallica's "One," trying to capture its podopercussive fury, but it still came out sluggish, as if I were playing with hotdogs taped to my fingers. Then there were lines in the one hand that didn't sync up with lines in the other, and I could almost hear a fan spin up in my cerebrum as grey matter began melting. It was as if Bach were indifferent to his students' agony, or perhaps wanted to present a rigorous final exam. I practiced certain sequences over and over, until my fingers felt like they would fall off and I couldn't go on, which I came to think of as my Schumann days (as opposed to the Wittgenstein variety), since Schumann had given his ring finger for a wife, little Clara, wrecking it to please her father, who was an ogre of a piano teacher. But playing the instrument also compelled me to wade deeper into the music, to get under its skin, which was the joy of it. I stumbled onto "walking bass," in which the left hand strolls down the keyboard at a deliberate pace, hand in pocket whistling, insouciant, oblivious to what the right hand does, with occasional switchbacks to gain altitude; or sometimes these maneuvers reminded me of throwing a typewriter carriage back in order to start clacking away on a new line. It was a technique we mostly associate with jazz now, giving Bach's music a strange, hip feel once you notice.

My progress throughout this period was haphazard and unpredictable. For long stretches, I seemed to be getting incomprehensibly worse, despite my fervent practice. I couldn't tell if this was because my standards were rising, whether I simply wasn't registering how far I had come, or whether I really was deteriorating. This was especially worrying in view of Bach's love of retrograde motion, whereby a theme would be stated first forward, then backward, and then perhaps forward *and* backward layered on top of one another, sometimes in a never-ending Möbius strip, as in the piano pieces of the *Musical Offering*. Perhaps I had heard too much of this retrograde motion, and now my technique was regressing, as well. When I mentioned the idea that I was somehow getting worse to Christopher, using an offhand ironic banter, he enthusiastically—almost zealously—seized on this possibility and emphasized how serious the situation was, that with my slovenly habits and poor technique nothing was more likely than my retrogressing. I lay awake at night pondering this possibility. I was uncertain which was worse—actually to decline in my performance, or to get better, but at a rate always outstripped by my rising standards, so that I would always feel like a failure no matter how proficient I became.

I came to suspect that had Bach had played an elaborate prank in ending the two-part inventions on the B minor. After getting the student acquainted with playing in two parts, and fooling him into thinking that difficulty corresponds to the number of voices, the last point was that this isn't so. A structurally simpler piece can be much harder to play than one that is far more complex. If it comes to that, a virtuosic line in a single hand can be next to impossible. The student begins playing Bach focused on the intellectual difficulties of playing, the sense that the brain is melting, but there are also the difficulties of the hand. A pianist with his brain transplanted into the head of a cobbler couldn't play at all; his mind would issue commands that his muscles, nerves, and tendons wouldn't carry out.

As I sank deeper into the music, explaining my obsession with the piano to others became more difficult. It was hard to convey how much I cared about Bach, and why achieving those serpentine rhythms of the B minor was now a life-defining endeavor. (I pictured my current epitaph: "He managed to progress from *so-so* to *below average*.") When I did try to explain, people quickly lost interest and changed the subject. A virtuoso who keeps up his craft and entertains the dinner guests with Chopin is someone you're excited to see; an adult beginner who taps around a bit between changing diapers is anodyne, perhaps even adorable. But middle-aged people who develop a mania for a subject they're unlikely to master and which is kept entirely private just seem odd.

I had started playing less for Lauren once I noticed how reluctantly she listened, and I avoided playing for family as much as possible. Something about the idleness in their requests for recitals bothered me, the lack of respect for the music itself. At school, no one cared, except for the occasional student who played, whom I would generally ply for information and treat like royalty. And yet, playing for myself became more and more important. I started to rise early so I could practice an hour or two before work, irritated that I had to trundle off eventually and confront the pointless emails, the reluctant students, the faculty meetings about how there was no money and how we had to implement Learning Outcome Assessments. By contrast, playing five notes on the white keys over and over to learn to apply exactly even pressure seemed deeply meaningful. Eventually, even those exercises that I'd shunned came to give me a sense of gratification deeper than anything else I did—they combined a tactile sensuality with the satisfying pain of flossing one's teeth.

Playing the piano thus produces a sense of interiority, as long as it isn't spoiled by competing for prizes, or playing for one's parents, or for some other purpose beyond the music itself. Instrumental music shouldn't be instrumental. Without this interiority, we lack a vital sadness, the melancholy monologue that sustains us as the others mewl and bray—Thoreau's true self that we find in solitude at ponds and pianos. Without it there is no music or poetry in our lives, let alone our books and records. And yet how often is our playing subordinated to pleasing the teacher, our relations, some other minder. Our whole lives are spent enmeshed in bureaucracies that test and monitor our progress—school, exams, grades, work, feedback, mentoring, hektoring, blind refereeing, external evaluation, tenure review, post-tenure review, student evaluation ("Why i didn't get an A i worked soo hrd ?!?!"), disability training, sexual harassment training, software training, noncognitive-skills training, anti–implicit bias training. Let there be some distant island of the mind unspoilt and unkept, a little omphalos of the world that the others cannot reach, where we dream our little dream—until it is time to enter the machine again, to mesh against the gears, to break upon the wheel.

4

The Man

I nevitably, my hand problems returned, and for a while
they seemed to be back for good. I kept practicing,
but I could only keep up a little with what I had learned
without making any further progress. Instead of playing,
I decided to learn more about Bach, and I began reading
the usual biographies. But these all began by saying that
nothing was really known about him, and everyone I
talked to about it seemed to think that his life was terribly
dull, hardly worth reading about. When I tried to persuade
Christopher otherwise, he clapped me on the shoulder and
said he was sure it was "some real white-knuckle stuff."
The biographers seemed embarrassed by this dullness,

conceding that the primary materials consisted mostly of receipts and ledgers, and often they rushed forward to discuss the music itself, or concentrated merely on his supposed genius, all of which gave the impression Bach was essentially an anonymous church mouse.

But these views turned out to be doubly wrong. In the first place, many people seemed to forget that Bach walked around armed with a sword and got into at least one knife fight or close enough (apparently pretty common among Baroque musicians, considering Handel very nearly died in a *duel* he held *during* an opera that he was *conducting*), that Bach spent hard time in prison and seems to have written some of his greatest music in the clink, that he routinely skipped work for weeks at a time in order to hike across the country to hear other musicians (to the great consternation of his employers), that he participated in dramatic organ duels against other virtuosos, at least when the French ones didn't run away, that he would stay up all night drinking and smoking while composing music for a job interview the next morning, that he fathered twenty children and wed two wives, that he vied with Frederick the Great, who attempted to impugn his musicianship toward the end of Bach's life, and that he died (more or less) while composing *The Art of Fugue*, the greatest work of counterpoint ever created. Who could consider such a life dull?

But even setting aside these details, the musty receipts and ledgers, far from being trivial, were in fact revelatory, just as a "dry" piece like the Minuet in G minor was in fact an X-ray of the soul in love. The ledgers catalogued what Bach read, what he ate, what he complained about, what he spent his money on, what work he did, who his employers were, what his ambitions were, what his students thought of him, how much he loved Anna Magdalena, his second wife, how much she loved yellow carnations, how much they worried about the prodigal, Johann Gottfried, who shamed Bach after he got him his first job, how there was never enough money, and yet somehow always just enough—and how much they all loved coffee. It would perhaps be comparable to having someone's complete browser history without knowing much else about them; in a sense this would be a very incomplete record, but in another sense this would tell you far more than superficially vivid accounts from friends and relatives might—accounts inevitably colored by vanity, or jealousy, or selective self-presentation. People, after all, are mostly the same, in their minds as much as their genes, and what matters is the one percent difference, and the receipts can tell us as much about that as anything else.

We see this in a single sentence from an obscure letter Bach wrote to the King of Poland complaining about the details of his work and pay:

> Whereas, however, Most Gracious King and Elector, a Worshipful University has expressly required that I furnish the music for the Old Service, and has accepted me for it, and I have

until now performed this office; whereas the salary that has been attached to the directorship of the New Service was never previously connected with the latter but specifically with the Old Service, just as the direction of the New Service at its inception was connected with the Old Service; and whereas, while I did not wish to dispute the directorship of the New Service with the organist of St. Nicholas's, yet the withdrawal of the salary, which, in fact, always belonged to the Old Service even before the New was instituted, is deeply disturbing and slighting to me: and whereas Church Patroni are not in the habit of changing the disposition of the regular compensation earmarked and provided for a servant of the Church, either by withdrawing it entirely or by decreasing it, in spite of which I have had to perform my office in respect to the above-mentioned Old Service for over two years already without compensation—accordingly my most obedient prayer and entreaty goes forth to Your Royal Majesty and Serene Electoral Highness that Your Majesty may issue most gracious commands that a Worshipful University at Leipzig shall leave the arrangement as it was formerly, and grant me the directorship of the New Service in addition to the directorship

of the Old, and particularly the full compensation for the Old Service and the incidental
fees accruing from both. [1]

Biographers who don't place this sentence at the very
core of their analysis can be safely dismissed, for what
doesn't one learn from such a sentence? Infinitely more,
surely, than from reverential speculations on "the nature
of genius" or "the sources of creativity."

One starts off thinking of Bach as gliding through
rococo palaces amid tinkling keyboards, and periwigs and
knee socks, but that's not how it was at all. I began to see
an apartment full of students in Leipzig, with children
running everywhere, full of life and noise, a wife trying
to keep order, and more abstractly, I saw the need for
money. Here was the greatest musician in history, shoving
away a draft of the E minor partita so he could write this
complaint, at once necessary to support his wife and seven
children (if we include little Christian Gottlieb!), not to
speak of other interlopers, and yet a complaint that was
petty and ridiculous in its own way, and absurdly incongruous with the music he was creating. More than that,
there was the sense of betrayal in the tone of the complaint,
the sense of being cheated by those who had promised a
decent income despite a lousy salary through incidental
fees which they were now siphoning away. Then there was
the *disrespect*—he was being "slighted," as if one could do
whatever one wanted with the church cantor, as if he were

some vulgar entertainer. And there was the hierarchy in the background to the letter, which required obsequious forms of address even when demanding simple justice, and which implied a series of fiefdoms and accompanying power struggles over their control and influence. Finally, I could feel the fury that all of these things combined must have elicited, even amid all the noise (and the smell!) of the screaming students who lived and studied all around, and the unimaginable crush of work composing and arranging music for Sunday at three different churches, just five days from now, and finishing his first published work of music, the partitas, which had to be perfect, and teaching students, rehearsing with performers, and raising the healthy children with Anna, burying the dead ones, and nursing sickly Christiana. (Way in the background I could hear Anna practicing at the keyboard with the new notebook Bach had just made for her, later inscribed "AMB 1725," her professional soprano still fine when she sang along, her fourth child almost beginning to show.) Amid all this sat Bach at his desk, a man of many turns, fighting the bureaucracy in an absurd letter there was no time for; proud, bitter, and desperate for money.

None of this seemed the least bit dull to me. The problem was that we tend to think of a life in chronological terms, and by the time we finish marching from one episode to the next, from one job posting or musical landmark to the next, we have forgotten what matters, if we are still reading at all. I came to see that Bach's life needed to be organized thematically instead, like a piece of music.

What struck me first was the sadness of it all: to be an orphan at ten, to live with a brother who locks you out of his music collection, to fend for yourself as a professional organist at eighteen, unable to study at the university—this was how it began for Bach. And at the other end of life it was the same theme played in reverse, having buried a wife and eleven children (including the prodigal), blinded and butchered by the same charlatan who operated on Handel's eyes, dead at sixty-five before he could finish *The Art of Fugue*. And the disrespect never ended: the city council with which he had ceaselessly quarreled wouldn't wait for his death, and started holding tryouts for his replacement as he still lay sick, and even then they passed over his son in their selection—a strange irony when Bach himself had such a keen eye for moribund musicians, whom he would replace with his sons or his students. Then all his goods were inventoried and disposed of—we have the ledgers—and he was dumped into an unmarked grave, and Anna had to apply for welfare, her sons doing little to support her, and she died at fifty-nine. Some of those kids became famous musicians in their own right, but there is something dreary in their dedication to the streamlined style that left Bach's counterpoint behind, paving the way to Haydn and Mozart, from the byways of Thuringia to

Vienna and glory. The prodigal died, and what was far worse, Johann Christian got lost in Italy and turned Catholic. (Imagine, a Catholic Bach!) Meanwhile, Papa Bach's music disappeared, a tiny fragment of it published, but vast monuments like *The Well-Tempered Clavier* still only in manuscript, and much of it lost forever like Aristotle's treatise on comedy, and other works sold for the value of the paper—to wrap cheese in the legend, but what does it matter whether the stink of it was cheese or fish?

And what happened in between all that? Mostly a great deal of humiliation. He was, to be sure, appreciated as a virtuoso organist and acquired fame throughout Germany and beyond as a performer. And in narrower circles, some of his music was well known for pedagogical purposes; Beethoven and Chopin both made their early reputations with the Bach they grew up practicing. But most people thought he was just another musician, one among many, and far from the best. When he applied for the post at Leipzig, at the height of his powers, he was their reluctant third choice, and even then he was supposed to teach the children Latin on the side. Whom did they really want? Who else but *Telemann*, whose mediocre essence had long since propelled him to glory, and if not him then at least Graupner. In part this was Bach's own fault. He had neither interest nor talent in self-promotion, and couldn't afford to publish much of his work, which no one would have bought anyway. Nowadays he would be the infelicitous artist who fails to have ten thousand followers on social media, and who doesn't insist that every conversation revolve around his work. And Bach lacked elite status, particularly in the form of a university degree. One might imagine no one would care whether an organist or cantor or Kapellmeister of all people wore this papered prestige, but this would mistake humanity in general and Germans in particular. Telemann and most of the other elite musicians had degrees, but Bach, the orphan boy, had gone straight to work. This status anxiety gnawed away at him, and coming in third place as the greatest musician in the world can only have confirmed his fears. Accordingly, he agonized over job titles and wrote scraping letters begging for more of them.

Music criticism had just been invented. Strangely, the inventor was Johann Mattheson, the duelist who came within a button's breadth of murdering Handel before he got to write the *Messiah*. The two were actually good friends, and they had once taken a merry trip north to Lübeck to try out as replacements for the great organist Buxtehude, only to discover that marrying the old man's old daughter was part of the deal (just as Buxtehude had gotten the job by taking *his* predecessor's daughter off *his* hands). A teenage Bach was also eager to hear Buxtehude, but he missed this merry confab by two years, since he had to walk hundreds of miles where the others arrived in a carriage to hear the great man play—and gaze upon his daughter and despair. Years later, Mattheson noted Bach's talents but also mocked him mercilessly. Imagine proud-but-anxious Bach's feelings on reading Mattheson's parody of his cantatas:

> "I, I, I, I had much grief, I had much grief, in my heart, in my heart. I had much grief, etc., in my heart, etc., etc., I had much grief, etc., in my heart, etc., I had much grief, etc., in my heart etc., etc., etc., etc., etc. I had much grief, etc., in my heart, etc., etc." Then again: "Sighs, tears, sorrow, anguish (rest), sighs, tears, anxious longing, fear and death (rest) gnaw at my oppressed heart, etc."[2]

But wait, this was no parody, but rather an appallingly accurate transcription of Bach's Cantata BWV 21. Nor was Mattheson the last critic; others published far more scathing indictments of the music itself, and once again on grounds that were in part accurate. Bach perfected a style that was already going *out* of style in his lifetime—dense, imitative counterpoint—and critics wrote humiliating jibes at his antique manner, devoid of emotion they said, burdened with boring technicalities. He had every reason to think his style of music would be abandoned by his own children, which it largely was, and that posterity would look on him as a curiosity, which many did. (Wagner: "Bach's musical language relates to that of Mozart and ultimately that of Beethoven as the Egyptian Sphinx relates to Greek sculpture: just as the human face of the Sphinx struggles to emerge from the body of the beast, so Bach's noble head labors to emerge from under his powdered wig."[3]) He spent his last ten years erecting monuments to a disappearing past that he must have imagined as Shelley or Marvell, standing alone in vast deserts of eternity.

And always—always—there was the money. Where was the ancillary income he had been assured? My hand problems persisted, and as I read ever deeper into the biographies and primary sources, I became more invested in his difficulties. In his letters, Bach complains bitterly about the "health wave" that overtook Leipzig at some point, meaning fewer funerals requiring his music, and I wept in sympathy at the consequent decline in his incidental fees. And it wasn't just funerals—the wedding situation was just as dire. For there were those citizens who thought it decent to marry *outside* of Leipzig to save some money, once again depriving Bach of most necessary income. Thank heavens his complaints succeeded, and these base fee-evaders were forced to pay him wherever they married, whether or not they actually needed his services.

In between all this melancholy there were joys, islands of light flickering in the darkness. His home was a "beehive," full of visiting musicians and students who worshipped him. He hated reluctant pupils, like some of those the city wished him to instruct, who had little interest in music or respect for him, but he lavished attention on more dedicated students, spending hour after hour with them as they noted in their letters home; and when he couldn't take their wrong notes anymore he would play through the entire *Well-Tempered Clavier* for them (sometimes several times) so they could learn by sympathetic resonance. At the end he wrote letters of recommendation that students must have feared—laconic, clipped paragraphs, hardly effusive but sincere and true. Eventually one of them was even worthy of marrying his daughter Elisabeth, another trick he learned from old Buxtehude. And there were the yellow carnations for Anna, who loved gardening so, and the abundant casks of wine he received from friends and relatives (except that sometimes he was responsible for the taxes and fees, payable on receipt, which he was sure to point out to his imprudent benefactor). And there was teaching Anna at the keyboard—Anna, who helped with the endless copying of music that eventually blinded Bach. Blinded: did he teach her the way Milton, another blind master, taught his daughters to pronounce Greek aloud but not to understand the words, since they didn't need to? Surely not! Bach needed his wife's help, but no one could read that notebook their family made and think of Milton—the notebook written in her soprano clef that contained the *Goldberg* aria, one imagines because Anna liked it so. And amid carnations and brandy and coffee and smoking the edifying pipe there was much joy apart from the dead children and the endless humiliation. But most of all one thinks of the family reunions of all the musical Bachs, a vast network dispersed far and wide, and there they would sing bawdy songs and improvise and drink and laugh, and it cannot be a coincidence that these great parties are all rolled up and stuck into the last of Anna's *Goldberg Variations*, the quodlibet, a mash-up of two folk tunes just as he played them at those parties:

> I've been away from you so long—get, get,
>   get over here!

> Beets and cabbage have driven me away,
> If Mother had cooked some meat I might
>   have stayed!

The last variation before the return to the aria thus evokes love and family and absence and homecoming—the *nostoi* of the musical Bachs and of the aria itself—and everyone's laughter, surely, as they slowly realized what was happening, the brilliance of the harmony, the incongruity between doggerel and craftsmanship, Bach's catalogue of ships, the joy of music and love and of life itself.

But here, too, there lurks a sadness, as there does behind all the major works he wrote. What, after all, was the purpose of the *Variations* but to put some aristocrat to sleep? A Russian count was said to have commissioned the work so that Goldberg could play them for him during his bouts of insomnia—all that work, well paid to be sure, for a soporific, specifically composed *not* to be heard, to be slept through! And earlier there was the Chaconne in

D Minor for solo violin, whose puzzling proportions and existential despair briefly became clear when I read that it was composed just after his first wife died while he was abroad and couldn't save her. The Chaconne was her tomb, a solo instrument playing polyphony, a single, grieving line in search of the voices that were lost; there was a set of variations for each wife. (Unfortunately, this appears to be another of the many myths that killjoy scholars are forever stamping out: "False! False!" they cry, as if to unweave the counterpoint.) And *The Well-Tempered Clavier* seems to have been written partly while imprisoned, since his employers in Weimar threw him in jail when he wanted to take another job, the ultimate non-compete clause. There are those who refer to this work as the Old Testament of the piano, which makes one think of Luther penned up in the Wartburg in Bach's hometown of Eisenach, translating the Bible and writing all those chorales that Bach would set, just as Bach sat in his jail cell translating his music into every key.

And so the naïve listener approaches Bach searching for signs of the sublime, while the connoisseur—sadder, wiser—listens for signs of the diminution in Bach's incidental fees and for the machinations of the bureaucracy, a dissonant chord signifying a health wave or a marriage outside the city limits, a stretto indicating the many letters required to settle some dispute with the consistory. If music carried its true meaning on its sleeve, instead of letting us project one all our own, however distant from the thoughts and feelings that inspired what we now convert to private uses, who knows if we should wish to listen at all?

⚜

Eventually I regained the use of my right hand and resumed playing. Christopher urged me to start over, to focus on the fundamentals, and to abandon my strict regimen of Bach. Mozart and his scales, he suggested, would show me the way. If you cannot play a scale you cannot play anything else, and I was keenly aware that my scales were all crooked and wrong. The problem was mostly concentrated in my right ring finger. When I played upward from thumb to middle finger all was normal, but my ring finger balked. Instead of depressing smoothly, it jutted out, stiff and straight, and slapped down on the key.

Studying Mozart felt at first like worshipping false gods, burning incense to Baal, a delay in achieving my great goal of playing the Fugue in C Minor. I began with the venerable Sonata in C Major K. 545, and felt guilty for every moment not spent with Bach. I could see the music only through the lens of counterpoint, and everything seemed wrong. The right hand played a pretty melody, but what on earth was the left hand doing? It merely alternated between two or three notes to fill out a chord, Alberti bass. Effectively, the left hand just played a single chord in the measure, while the right hand sang its soprano.

Where was the counterpoint? Why did the left hand just sit there without contributing? And why were there only two voices to begin with? It was as if a Roman legion, with its three lines of maniples, had marched into battle but left behind the grizzled veterans, the triarii, who shamed and backstopped all the rest.

In a way, the situation reminded me of Bach's conducting. It is said that when he led the orchestra, he had a far more kinetic approach than today's genteel conductors, who are rather passive when one thinks about it. If anything is amiss, they remain chained to their podiums, stabbing at the air in vain. Bach, by contrast, would wander among the musicians yelling at them to set them straight (*Kippelfagottist!*), and if something was lacking he wasn't afraid to add it himself. In fact, his keyboard players had to accustom themselves to seeing master Bach's arms slowly sliding in from behind in order to add additional lines of music improvised on the spot. (It is these reach-around harmonies that one begins to fill in listening to his solo compositions.) And after a while, when we listen to the meager, thinned-out music of other composers, the polyphobic efforts of an Aaron Copland, say, one starts to imagine Bach silently approaching the piano from behind, and inserting another three or four voices to the mix so as to flesh out the harmony. Listening to Bach slowly alters how we hear everything else, making it seem unfinished and insubstantial. So I felt initially, sitting down to the idols of Mozart.

But that melody! I had heard it ten thousand times before—everyone has—but playing it in the flesh I suddenly felt its power. Bach on the piano is the sound of eternity, not of the Baroque, but this was another order of eternity, not just beyond accidents of time and place, of the random fads of 18th-century Vienna, but inevitably perfect and perfectly inevitable. It was music carved from silence like the statue from the stone; this was the true Parthenon. One could imagine Bach offering many variations on the fugues, different lines of counterpoint, and in fact he always continued to improve on his earlier works, but it was impossible to imagine a change to Mozart, any more than we can imagine a classical column's fluting changed from vertical to horizontal.

And the sheer joy of it! Those descending scales connecting the first and second themes, and above all the passage concluding the arpeggios that follow (balancing the scales)—the whinnying, the neighing in those grace notes leading up to the trill, which one can only compare to the moment when a dog has been told that he is a very, good, boy, and that he is going for a WALK, while his master grabs the jangling leash, and the beast paws at the door whinnying wildly, and therein displays a purity of all-consuming happiness that grownups are entirely incapable of, canine happiness being as superior to human happiness as canine love is superior to human love.

To my consternation, I found myself weeping when I played this ridiculous music that was not Bach, which

I found rather alarming. What was next? Would I end up playing Chopin and all those other bed-wetters? Was there a distant future in which I lost my identity altogether and began listening to *Puccini*? But Christopher was right. It was a world of childlike purity that I expected to hate or make fun of, but instead found myself melting into. I thought back to Sunday school and Jesus's bewildering insistence that we must become as children again. How was this possible after all the sleazy grown-up things the world made you do, after all the callous things I'd said to Mother before she died, or to Lauren, whom I still refused to marry after sixteen years? In Mozart there seemed to be an answer. It made you think we might recover all the wisdom we lost growing up, and that you could change the past like Gatsby, that nothing was beyond redemption.

Next to all this dolor, Bach's Germanness seemed most salient to me. Commentators avoid this theme (or paw at it gingerly from a distance, with an academic's stick), fearing to be associated with the puerile nationalism of the 19th century and later the Nazis, but it is obvious that there is something distinctively German about Bach. It isn't a coincidence that counterpoint was perfected in Thuringia (where Bach was born) and Saxony (where he died) and not in Venice. If this makes us uncomfortable, we should reflect on both the good and the bad of it, the sublime search for order and architectonic that links Bach and Immanuel Kant, as well as the penchant for the ridiculous, the obsession with official titles and breaches of etiquette, the incidental fees, the rule-mongering, the absence of French elegance or English wit, the sense of humor that keeps its distance like an unscrupulous relation who owes you money. Only Germany could have produced Bach, but no German could have been Degas or Oscar Wilde. We might as well, then, recognize the rough overlap of country and culture, and the good and the bad, even if these are just traditions and archetypes, and perhaps fading of late.

The French talent for whimsy and grace, for a light touch, makes the most striking contrast. The pâtissier makes effortless pastry puffs; the Saxon brings his beer stein slamming down. The French artist pirouettes along a rope; Bach is often brilliant, but also lumbering and full of the (false) appearance of effort. A certain dense, forbidding texture pervades, a dough kneaded by stout maidens with their sleeves rolled up, suited to dark breads that are wholesome and last a hard winter, but nothing to serve Degas's ballerinas with champagne. One sees this even in the titles. French keyboardists are full of play: Couperin has The Flatterer, The Butterflies, The Grapepickers, or the very best, Le Tic-Toc-Choc. A whole subspecies appears dedicated to amorous conquests: The Spanish Girl, The Frisky One, The Bold One, The Dangerous One—and then, The Regrets. And it wasn't just Couperin; Rameau had titles like The

Gathering of Birds or The Sensitive One. Isn't it all fun! Bach, on the other hand, had titles like Ricercar a 3, or Passacaglia and Fugue in C Minor, or *Die Clavier-Übung*, which contained all those suites that aped the French dance moves, like teenagers tottering under the disco ball during the slow dance. Meanwhile, in Italy Vivaldi evokes spring and all its happy delights:

> Springtime has come to us.
> Birds greet her festively with a glad song,
> And springs by the breath of gentle breezes
> With sweet murmuring run.

In Bach we get:

> Repentance and regret, repentance and regret
> Grind the sinful heart in two.

The French are cool, at least in Paris, at least for Europeans; Bach fundamentally is not. Trying hard isn't cool, and there is no way to write counterpoint without *looking* like you are trying, even if you are good enough to do it effortlessly.

We notice this in other disciplines, as well. The philosopher Schopenhauer once tried to offer an example of something *funny*:

> If we consider that, for an angle, two lines are
> required to meet, which, when lengthened,

intersect, while the tangent touches the circle only at a point, but at this point is strictly parallel to it, and if we keep the relevant abstract conviction in mind that an angle between the arc of a circle and the tangent is an impossibility—while yet such an angle lies before us on a piece of paper—this will readily force a smile on us.[4]

Such, such is the great professor's idea of funny—he will *force* us to smile. Admittedly, this is only supposed to illustrate the lower degrees of hilarity, preparing the way for the real rib-ticklers to come, but even so it reads like a parody of the labored search for wisdom, an example only of meta-humor.

One shouldn't exaggerate these differences, of course. Plenty of the preludes in *The Well-Tempered Clavier* whip and tingle (that B-flat major in Book I!); many of *The Goldberg Variations* laugh and sing; walking bass can sound like jazz. Bach, the East German *Ossi*, isn't some hipster, but neither is he square. The *Goldberg* theme, for instance, is subtly varied, and in general almost hidden from view, unlike, say, Pachelbel's idiotic canon that repeats the same little figure over and over, and one hears the laughter in *Goldberg*'s beets and cabbages toward the end. But on the whole, you can't help think of that arc encompassing Kant and Kiefer and Wagner and *Wings of Desire*, mostly laughless, but profound in its rigor and intellectually superior. And in Bach, at least, there are the characteristic virtues and obsessions that lie behind (sometimes *far* behind) that arc—craft, duty, guild, industry, order, precision, punctuality, contract, receipt, inspection, and review. These could produce results that were almost cruel, as when Bach insisted that his cousin pay for a copy of the *Musical Offering*, or in his stoical letters for his students, but they could also prompt feats of abnegation, as when Bach was called upon to inspect (of course) an organ constructed by Johann Scheibe, whose son had derided his music in print. He nevertheless declared the organ flawless—if only after "the strictest examination that an organ was perhaps ever subjected to."[5] In love these virtues manifest themselves in a certain indefatigable quality we can see in those twenty children, and in a deep loyalty—it is impossible to imagine Bach having an affair. Status is important to maintaining order, and so this plays its role as well; it is visible on the title page of his first publication, where he describes himself as the *Hochfürstlich Sächsisch-Weissenfelsischen wirklichen Capellmeistern und Directore Chori Musici Lipsiensis*, which there really isn't any point in translating from the several languages evidently required to explain how important he was, except to note that something similar persists to this very day, so that one must undergo extensive training to address German business associates, using formalities that Americans find bewildering and absurd ("Very honored Mr. Doctor Schmidt, I am writing to invite you . . ."). Debussy captures all of this from his French perspective in complaining about "the old Saxon cantor"—that "his prodigious technical skill . . . is not enough to fill the terrible void created by his insistence on developing a mediocre idea no matter what the cost!"[6] But he leaves out, of course, the payoff from this thoroughness that emphasizes order over wit, and technique over inspiration. Sometimes one wants a beer stein to smash that little pastry puff.

Then there is the disastrous Italian captivity, when Bach discovered Vivaldi and the rest. The French influences are felt primarily in the dance forms of the suites and partitas, and in pompous overtures, whereas the Italian captivity can be seen in orchestral work like the *Brandenburg Concertos*, and in Bach's weird attempts at Church opera in the Passions. There is a sense, of course, in which all European music—indeed, all of Europe—is the product of Italy. There is Palestrina's polyphony, Monteverdi's opera and the sing-songy recitative, the key development of monody, in which the music is focused on a central melody (as opposed to the beautiful but unhummable pap of Palestrina), the rise of purely instrumental music in Corelli, the orchestra, and on and on. Even the organ tradition is rooted in musicians like Frescobaldi and Italian forms like the toccata. But we can distinguish the general background from the more particular turn toward Italy when Bach began working at Weimar, ensconced at his small but lofty organ in the chapel called the "heavenly castle," with access to a good—an all *too* good—music library.

What then is so bad about the captivity? The cliché, after all, is that Bach absorbed the various national styles and then synthesized them into a product everybody loves. But consider the *Brandenburg Concertos*, which represent everything most appalling about the Baroque, the age of the gaudy golden frill. (When you travel around Europe and come to a church described as a "Baroque masterpiece," run for your life.) To begin with, the concertos are almost always performed with a harpsichord, which is intrinsically offensive. In order to be fair, one must consider only versions with a piano, which critics and visiting assistant professors will of course consider inauthentic, since they prefer the authentically bad to the inauthentically good. But there is no escaping the recorder, another horrifying appurtenance of the Baroque, whose presence always signals that dullness and men in stockings are nigh. (Who has ever had their heart ripped out by anything involving the recorder?) Even substituting a flute doesn't help, since we've all now heard a million versions with the recorder and formed the appropriate impressions. Perhaps it is merely the association with Telemann, but turning on the radio and hearing the twittering of recorders can only suck the life force out of you.

In fact, it is the twittering cheerfulness of the concertos that makes them so discouraging. There are, to be sure, more specific features one might object to: the thinned-out polyphony; the tedious alternation between the tutti of the orchestra and the soloists in ritornello form; the hippity-hoppity rhythms intended to sparkle like frilly palaces; the melodic contours drawn from a southern idiom that fears counterpoint. What is best in the concertos is the invention of the piano concerto in No. 5, which we enjoy precisely as a keyboard work, and for the respite from all that fiddling. But fundamentally, it is the relentless desire to *please* that makes these Italianate pieces so dismaying. They are composed to charm the chattering wigs and frocks in the hall, much like the polite Viennese music that followed. You can *feel* their eagerness to ingratiate, the desire not to insult or challenge. How different from the great keyboard works aimed at fellow musicians! How different, too, from the lugubrious *St Matthew Passion*, whose subject matter enabled Bach to set aside niceties. The concertos are the artist learning to scrape and bow, begging to be a member of the club, music for a margrave. They represent all of us learning to get on in the world, to conceal our sullenness when we walk out the front door. Bach sets all six pieces in the major key lest anyone feel put out, just as we smile and simper when we would glower; they are PR memos next to the private confessions at the keyboard.

Some are shocked by the very idea that any of Bach's works could be flawed. If it comes to that, there are many who think classical music in general is wonderful, and that anyone who doesn't enjoy a major work or composer or period is simply ignorant. Enthusiasts respond angrily that critical views are "subjective" or "merely your opinion," as if the devotee's more catholic tastes were any less a matter of opinion. The truth is that the further out we zoom from the particular piece to an artist's entire catalog, to a historical period, to a genre, to human culture in general, the less defensible enthusiasm becomes, and the greater the likelihood that we are succumbing to some form of invisible indoctrination. Artists are merely the vehicles for their works. And so much must go right for a book or movie to be any good, the odds are always against it coming off, and so from a purely statistical point of view there is really no chance that most or all of someone's work will be great. We all regress toward mediocrity. It is only piano teachers, assistant professors, and other apparatchiks of the Museum who persuade us that Bach (Shakespeare, da Vinci . . .) in general must be worthwhile—let's organize one more conference, let's have one more recital.

Cultural maturity is always presented as the process of becoming *more* appreciative, perhaps because mass society is so unappreciative to begin with, but sometimes it is musical *dis*appreciation that we need. We may convey a great deal in being discriminating and explaining to our kids why something is bad or just mediocre. There is nothing more deadening than to teach that one may not dislike any of Homer's poetry or Bach's music. What is important are the reasons for these reactions, and whether they reflect seasoned judgment or mere inexperience. Can, then, Bach be bad? A better question is whether Bach can be boring, or routine, or tedious, as Debussy says. It should be obvious what the answer to *that* question is, and the boring is always bad. There is no shame in it; even Wagner nods—think of those scenes in the *Ring* in which Wotan explains to characters the action we have just witnessed, punishing us with off-stage exposition of what we already know, which any sensible editor would cut. If we can roll our eyes at this, we can roll our eyes a bit at Bach as well, especially when we can blame it on the Italians.

But we still haven't reached the most Teutonic feature of Bach's life, the constant struggle with the bureaucracy. Germany has hardly been alone in this obsession; Russia has exhibited, if anything, a far more thoroughgoing passion for forms in triplicate and stamps in little green books. But it is the motive that counts. In Russia, the point of the bureaucracy is ultimately centralization and control; the impetus is outrage that you should imagine you could do anything without permission from on high. In Germany, by contrast, there exists a more noble enthusiasm for the bureaucracy in itself. "One must always treat the procedures as ends in themselves, never merely as a means." In either system, everything takes forever and nothing gets done (from a superficial American point of view), but at least in Germany your fervent pleas to mail your package without the form will be denied out of a sense of duty, and not with a base ulterior motive. Perhaps for this reason, Russians ridicule/celebrate their bureaucracy in writers like Gogol, but nothing quite compares to the portrayals in Kafka, a Bohemian who nevertheless reflects German culture. One thinks of the portrayal in *The Castle* of the clerks and their love of documents, their wild desperation when they run out of files to process, their envy of colleagues who are favored with more of them.

The dispute over pay quoted earlier culminated in a letter to the King of Poland, and yet this was just a tiff compared to the bureaucratic disputes to come. Bach's conflict with rector Ernesti, for instance, produced a vast correspondence over who got to appoint the leader of the little boys' choir, which Americans would not anticipate requiring (again!) a letter to the King of Poland. Bach was astonished—*astonished*—at the innovations the rector was attempting. There is talk of a "new departure," of "usurpation," "shame," "public humiliation," "encroachment," and "irreparable disorders." Ernesti in turn "cannot sufficiently express" *his* astonishment at the radical changes Bach is proposing in overlooking the rector's authority.[7] Bach first brings a complaint to the town council, followed by a second, a third, and a fourth complaint, before a copy of Ernesti's seven page rebuttal reaches him, resulting in a decree from the town council, which only provokes an appeal by Bach to the town consistory, followed by another, and then the inevitable letter to the King of Poland. One can practically hear the exasperation at the court, as some poor official remands the case back to the consistory, where, after yet further back and forth . . . the outcome is swallowed up by history, like the ark of the covenant in *Raiders of the Lost Ark*, as if the whole point were the bureaucratic machinations in themselves, not the insignificant outcome. The tale reminds us of Kafka, of Kleist, of tortured journeys past the tollhouses on the Rhine, except that one doesn't know whom to feel more sorry for, Bach being tormented by the bureaucracy, or the officials who had to endure the endless letters, filled with enclosures and exhibits. (Then again, who knows—perhaps Kafka was right about the almost sexual thrill of the dossier.) And after all that? Why, back to working on *The Goldberg Variations*, which presumably express as much about German bureaucracy as they do about love and nostalgia, just as Wagner's music is secretly about fleeing his creditors and seducing his patrons' wives.

It remains true that there is a universality in Bach that absorbs all and reflects it back in his own work, much more fully developed and magnified. In this he was unusual, and superior, perhaps in a distinctively German way. The French and Italians could have learned plenty from German musicians at the time, but there seem to be few who showed the level of interest in figures like Bach that Bach showed in them. The comparison may seem unfair—Vivaldi was famous in a way that Bach was not. But this begs the question, for his relative fame was in part the *result* of Germans celebrating Italians and the Italians ignoring the Germans. In any case, the impression of an asymmetry in curiosity, in the disinterested obsession with craft, and in cultural humility, remains. German Lutherans seem more interested in what Italian Catholics were up to than vice versa. Universality thus shows itself to be particular. But Bach's absorptions and magnifications distort as much as they magnify. Dance moves are not easily translated into Thuringian counterpoint, and so the disco ball twirls and we limp along. Not sensing all this, or perhaps not being able to stop oneself despite sensing it, is one last Germanism one finds in Bach.

For the better part of a year, I played almost nothing but Mozart's K. 545. Try as I might, I couldn't play the series of descending scales at the beginning of the piece fluidly. My right hand resembled a crab scuttling sideways, with one ragged claw—that ring finger—poking out the front; or sometimes my hand was an elephant blundering through the bush, its trunk flopping about uncontrollably. Mozart was the ultimate simplicity, but he exaggerated every little flaw.

It started to become clear that you don't really learn a new piece of music, you acquire new skills. Each new piece asks the student a fundamental question: Can you play arpeggios? Can you play a trill? Can you play counterpoint? K. 545 asks the simplest question of all: Can you play a C major scale? No black keys required, just the white ones. But to my exasperation, C major ended up being the hardest scale to play. There was nowhere for the fingers to hide, no little hill or crevice to conceal a small awkwardness, no change in hand configuration to offer flagging muscles a rest. It was just an endless sea of flat, undifferentiated white, like Moby Dick, whose terror consists in the whiteness of the whale. It should have been easy, but making the fingers, each different in length and strength, to land exactly flat was excruciatingly difficult, even now that I had learned some basic Bach, which didn't require the same skill, since there are few extended scales in Bach, and none so naked as in Mozart. And yet the music itself brought me endless joy. Playing thus involved a jarring incongruity between the divine innocence and elegance of the music, and my clumsy attempts to perform it, between the master's blueprint and the pile of rubble I built out of it.

I began focusing on my fingers more. Instead of looking at the keys or the music, I just stared into the mirror of the fallboard which reflected back my hands in black. At first, things looked all right, but eventually I saw that everything was wrong. My pinkies would fly out at acute angles; my second finger often over-rotated and skated across the key; the fourth finger flipped up instead of arcing. I was determined to get those clumsy American fingers, shaped by subway straps and soda cans, to curl gracefully around Mozart. After countless hours of philosophical analysis and observation I finally realized what I needed to do: I needed to push my fingers down from my hands onto the keys and then lift them back up again. Two years in, this was my great revelation. If it sounds ridiculous, all I can say is that before I wasn't doing this, not even trying, really. What I was doing was closer to clenching my fist against the piano. Changing my technique and readjusting everything seemed like a heroic task, though, especially since I found that once I'd learned some music, my technique was baked in; changing how I worked my hands in the present had no effect on how I played those earlier pieces, which I performed by reflex-action now. Just as Bach continually updated his manuscripts, adding additional lines and polishing the counterpoint, so the performer must continually revise in light of evolving technique, even if this means tearing everything up and starting all over again.

Christopher had always officially preferred Mozart to Bach. But he did so only in the exaggerated way that friends will highlight minor differences to generate creative tension. He would casually taunt the laborious quality of certain fugues, while I would remark on how vapid Mozart's serenades were. Sitting at the keyboard I would frantically text him for advice on my fingers, and whether out of generosity or because he hated smoking fish, he always replied. "Try playing at 50% tempo for the week," "Grab that low F with your thumb." When I described my confusion at being able to play some Bach tolerably well without mastering Mozart's scales, he replied, "That's okay, you'll just be a specialist ;-)". Of course, being a "specialist" in this sense just meant that I was incompetent, but it was his way of consoling me, drawing attention to my failures but playfully so it wouldn't smart. He excelled at this type of sensitivity, knowing just which note to strike and in which register to produce the desired effect. It was this that had interested me in him in the first place, lamenting Metallica's Black Album together in eleventh grade. He was Gatsbyesque in this seismic acuity—as well as in his money and tragic lack of pull-through. His homelife had been troubled in a suburban kind of way, and eventually amid all the screaming across those white carpets something just broke, and he lost his capacity for resilience; after a particularly brutal exchange at the conservatory he had bolted and never returned.

I sent these messages to him in the morning, while practicing before work. I had recently padded the small piano room with foam to reduce the sound levels, and in that stillness, despite my butchery, Mozart set me going like a conductor's baton, and the music buoyed me across all the straits of the day. It sustained me through the school's active learning program, whose premise was that students could no longer stay still for more than five minutes at a stretch, and that we were crazy to expect them to learn anything by listening to us and writing some things down; it sustained me through tenure cases, where we pondered whether so-and-so's sleeping his way through the graduate students and his complete disdain for teaching anyone anything were obstacles to tenure (certainly not! his journal articles were highly cited); it sustained me when Lauren and I fought and the universe contracted into a tiny ball and there was nothingness and death—it didn't matter next to the whinnying of Mozart that lit the way through the day's darkness like a glittering beam of joy.

A third theme sounded reading ever deeper into the Bach biographies. (Since his life is said to be uneventful, one might imagine these books to be short, but Philipp Spitta's 19th century brick runs to a thousand pages, and that's just the most famous.) Some would refer to this third theme as Bach's genius, but that is to beg all of the important questions; a better term to use would be "craftsmanship," though this isn't quite right, either. What we really want, to start with, is the notion of a *Fachmann*. A *Fachmann* is someone like a trained electrician you hire on grounds of their expertise, or a medical specialist you would consult, so something like a "professional" or an "expert." (*Fach* means subject, or field, or line of work.) But *Fachmann* also connotes the mastery of a craft in a way that "professional" doesn't quite—being a professional mostly just means that you are getting paid. "Professional" thus directs us toward remuneration, and "specialist" toward narrowness, whereas *Fachmann* suggests above all training and expertise. "Craftsman" or "expert" get us closer, but few electricians describe themselves as craftsmen or experts.

Fachmann has both positive and negative connotations. This is equally true of earlier versions of the idea, as in ancient Greek discussions of the *technikos*, also often translated as "craftsman" or "expert." The essential problem is that these terms point upward toward the brain, but also downward toward the hands; they involve domain knowledge and consequently expertise, but they also have an air of grubbiness about them, something banausic. No one who has a manager's responsibilities or who works in an intellectual field turns out to be a *Fachmann*. A CEO is not a *Fachmann*, nor is a theoretical physicist, even though each may know everything about his area. By contrast, a brilliant radiologist or experimental physicist working on complicated lab equipment may be. The *Fachmann*, moreover, works at someone else's direction, and the relevant schools are often specially designated, have lower entrance requirements, and the exams themselves serve as filters and gateways to the prestige professions. This very fact in turn produces egalitarian anxieties, efforts at reform, false promises to undo this social structure, and so on.

All of this goes back centuries. The concept of the *Fachmann* reflects an ancient memory of guilds, of journeymen, of complicated licensures, a praiseworthy obsession with craftsmanship mixed with a dubious desire to keep out rivals in order to maintain standards—and prices. By contrast, the American "professional" reflects a much shorter memory that goes back only to the industrial age, one that sides with consumers, so to speak, in their battle with overpriced guilds and unions. The professional isn't expected to be obsessed with his craft because he isn't treated as well, and because he is subjected to relentless price competition. My electrician must be decent or he will lose out to his rivals, but there is nothing in the American system to nurture an intrinsic interest in his field, an autonomous sense that he should be ashamed not knowing something, even if it doesn't pay to know.

Americans therefore possess neither the virtues nor the vices of the *Fachmann* system. The faint air of contempt for working with one's hands, of being restricted to a domain that others must supervise, is missing so long as you make a decent living. College is prized, but not because of anything you might learn there, only because of a certain dream or fantasy which is itself defined in crass, materialist terms. In America, it is the millionaire who needn't work at all who is ashamed at some Christmas party, while the self-made tinkerer is eager to reveal himself. But on the other hand, we Americans also lack the appreciation for expertise, and the training and learning behind it, that factor in the *Fachmann* concept. We are socially egalitarian in our attitudes if not in economic reality, and we are intellectual opportunists, all of which yields cheap but lousy wiring.

Bach wasn't a *Fachmann*, of course. A musical performer wouldn't be considered a craftsman, and a full-blown composer is too much of an artist to fit comfortably in the category, either. But while he chafed at any suggestion he was a performing drudge—a mere *musikant*—he eagerly pressed his claims to being a consummate master of his craft, and sought title after title to certify this fact, and later produced work after work to demonstrate it. If there was a technique at the keyboard Bach would know it, if there were musical innovations somewhere in some library he would find them, and he knew everything there was to know about the engineering of organs and of acoustics, to the point that he was hired to examine newly built organs like Scheibe's, and comment not just on their voicing but their metallurgy. He had techne, craft, art, the art of the fugue—a phrase and title that can only be understood in light of *Fachmann* culture and its web of associations. He even had his own guild in the network of Bachs across Germany who supported one another and held those reunions referenced in that beets-and-cabbage *Goldberg Variation*. And yet it is noteworthy that Bach never showed any interest in abstract theory. While he had at least implicit command of the intellectual subtleties of harmony, acoustics, and the rest, he never displayed any interest in formalizing this knowledge or in writing treatises about it. He was like the grandmaster who wins at chess over the board, but shows little interest in theory or endgame tables. In this, too, he was an artisan, focused on his hands at the keyboard, on what he could make, disinterested in knowledge for its own sake, in Aristotle's ideal of pure contemplation. Bach may not have been a *Fachmann* per se, but the obsession with craft and technique, independent of money or social prestige, are central to Bach's way, and emerge from the *Fachmann* cult.

When Americans contemplate art without the frame of techne, we tend to reach for *genius*, especially since we suffer from the influence of Romanticism without the medieval or Renaissance correctives. Europeans can view Wagner in light of Palestrina; Americans fundamentally cannot.

Our great artist isn't a craftsman, or anything close, but an inexplicable genius. Our kids play an instrument, but if they don't like it they stop, and it doesn't occur to us to (gently) beat them into excellence, unless we import that idea from some other tradition that immigrated with us. Our kids read or used to read *Moby-Dick*, but how often does the teacher explain the craft involved, let alone impose the training that would allow a student to acquire it? There are the exceptions—the modernist emphasis on technique, T. S. Eliot and Ezra Pound, *il miglior fabbro* and all that, but then they were turncoats. There are thirty times as many books on genius as there are on craftsmanship for sale.

Bach is still one half cathedral architect, semi-anonymous, self-effacing, concerned with expertise and the glory of God. No one told the builders of Chartres they were geniuses. But the artist as rock star is not far off; Beethoven, Paganini, Liszt, and the concert prima donnas are all lined up, and there is already glory to be had, in the opera at Hamburg, perhaps, like Handel, who was a kind of twin to Bach, representing the path not taken. Accordingly, there is no record anywhere of the slightest professional envy, disdain, condescension, or braggadocio (except to assuage his own status anxiety); everything speaks to professional curiosity and proper pride in his work, a modesty that one really only observes in those who are so capable that they have no need to hear themselves lauded or to see anyone else fail. For the same reason

Bach wasn't above continuously refining his own work, even when it was astonishing to begin with. Each piece is continuously polished and improved, recycled when appropriate, for nothing is ever finished. His music didn't come in a dream or an opioid stupor; it was an artifact forever to be remade in light of new needs, new technique and insight.

If Bach had merely been a genius, then the passing of his art would hardly matter. A genius perversely invents problems where there weren't any before, but problems it turns out we're happy to have. *Solving* the problems isn't the point. A genius is Plato failing in his *Republic* to explain why we should do the right thing when we could do wrong with impunity, or Wagner failing to agglomerate all of the arts into a never-ending melody. Genius requires seeing what no one else has seen and therefore is "wisdom and youth." But the master craftsman is superior to genius, for he creates the perfect artifact. Preferring genius to craftsmanship is to fetishize the process of creation over the work itself (a sure sign of callowness) and in the end it is the work that counts. It is all that counts.

Geniuses come and go; every age has its share. There will always be those who spontaneously, with little instruction, see peaks to climb, problems to surmount that no one else can. It is unfortunate to lose an Einstein or a Debussy, men who rely on private insight rather than public technique, but there will be more like them; science will march on without Einstein, one-off artists will sprout up like Debussy. But there won't be another Bach because the technique that he acquired has itself vanished. The master craftsman arises from a tradition like a high plains butte, and if the plains themselves disappear so do the peaks. The situation is like that of Homer, whom students imagine a genius scribbling in a cave somewhere on Mt. Olympus, when in fact he merely perfected a vast, existing body of oral poetry; he was an outgrowth, not a singularity. So Bach is Buxtehude and Vivaldi and Palestrina, only with a more perfect command of the art, Daedalus to the average craftsman of kites and corn mazes. The reason there won't be another Homer isn't that there aren't any comparable geniuses, but that there is no more tradition of Greek epic. Everything that lent sense to it—the absence of writing, the need for formulas and epithets to manage oral recitation, the distant memory of bronze age heroes—is simply gone. Likewise, Bach didn't seek to found some new tradition so as to escape an anxiety of influence. On the contrary, he reveled in his time and sought only to perfect what came before and make his own distinctive contribution. But now that tradition has itself disappeared.

Where and when should we expect to find the greatest musician of all time? It is hard to say, but surely not in the dismal forests of Thuringia in the 17th century, populated by a couple of tens of thousands dwelling in poverty. Greatness depends on talent, talent depends on a population base, on money, and on a suitable market, none of which favor 17th-century Thuringia. And yet the dismal forests of Grimm secreted Bach, while no one in a hundred years will remember much of our music, despite our having so many more people and resources to draw on. The real miracle isn't that we collectively invented Bach, but how quickly we uninvented him. (When you propose at a party that the human phenomenon of music peaked in 1750, plus or minus sixty years, everyone laughs, but when you ask them to name a time when there was genuinely better music they don't laugh as hard.) One has the haunting feeling that there must have been far greater musical talents since Bach's day who didn't produce simply because we didn't demand the right things. Musical training nowadays is directed toward a kind of museum-craft, toward perfecting the performance of the past, not toward independent creation. You can't help wondering: if we discarded our fossils, held competitions in polyphonic improv and in realizing figured bass, starting at ages ten or eleven, if we threw over the recorders and the *authentically* bad performances, could we nurse a little demand, yank the pull cord, and initiate a virtuous circle?

If not, our only hope for recapturing Bach's craft lies with machines. Some time ago our hopes would have lain with China or India or Japan, and in benefiting from their talents, but it is a remarkable fact that few societies seem to have shown much interest in systematic harmony, let alone counterpoint. If computers can teach themselves to play chess and master it in a minute through pattern recognition, what is to stop them from emulating musical styles and producing millions of additional fugues and symphonies? When they try (really try), will their efforts make Bach's star shine the brighter by their lame results, or embarrass him the way they embarrass our chess? Will they ever progress beyond throwing up possibilities that must be sifted by humans? Will they reach beyond imitating hallmarks to a higher level of generalization and produce something as original, say, as *The Goldberg Variations* or the invention of opera? And if they did, should we exult or despair?

The recapitulation of K. 545 begins in the "wrong" key of F, which Christopher claimed to have some complicated harmonic explanation, but which I attributed to the sheer beauty of the higher register. Somehow that eternal theme sounded all the more ethereal way up there (yet G would have been *too* high), and I felt even more aware of the ideal motion of fingers mimicking that sound: fronds of seaweed undulating in a morning's tide; yet when I tried to play that way everything felt stiff and harsh, like crampons puncturing the ice.

Christopher, meanwhile, kept moving the goalposts. I had learned some inventions? Congratulations, but of course no one could seriously claim to have "learned" something they couldn't play from any arbitrary point? ("Measure 17, fourth beat—go!") Naturally, I could perform each voice in each piece on its own, independent of the others? Did I practice *singing* each part accurately before touching the keys? And sometimes he would send me necromantic suggestions, like that I soak my arms in water for an hour before playing, or he would message me in the middle of the night that if I wasn't practicing at that *precise* moment I didn't want it badly enough. I began to respond with parody: "If you don't slather your body in anti-rheumatic honey you really don't care." It was never quite clear if he meant it, or if he was kidding around, or just out drinking. These exchanges reminded me that over time, a teacher becomes more of a coach, and then a motivator, and finally just a kindred spirit who can provoke you when you need it.

Christopher had been right that Mozart was a reality check, and in any case, I'd learned that Bach would have *loved* Mozart, which for some reason made a difference to me. Nothing could have shaken his confidence in his own approach to music, and no one could have made him anxious rather than just professionally curious, but he would have marked the craftsmanship of even simple music like 545. I could see exactly what he would have done stumbling onto the score in some time traveler's library—how he would have copied it and arranged it for other combinations of instruments, but modified with additional counterpoint; how it would briefly have influenced his own style markedly, and then with more nuance thereafter; and how he would have admired all of the new ideas it embodied and its *fachmännische* construction, without the slightest concern that it would eclipse his own work, which is all anyone else ever thinks about.

Mozart asks you to become a child again in more ways than one. In the twinkle-twinkle variations, for instance, he asks you to take seriously (but not *too* seriously!) a nursery rhyme and a few simple phrases so he can demonstrate how much there *is* in a phrase, and what the least of us may grow into, by way of analogy. Just as in 545, he asks us to set aside our grown-up pretensions, and accept a divine humility instead. And for students, Mozart is a figure like Socrates, who wasn't executed for saying things people didn't wish to hear—he said almost nothing at all—but for asking them to sing a Mozartian phrase, a simple little nursery rhyme: "I don't know!" This makes studying Mozart as an adult far superior, because the central lesson of recovering childhood's simplicity and humility, of Socratic ignorance, is one that children themselves cannot learn.

Mozart forced me to accept that I couldn't play eight notes in a row correctly. My hands no longer resembled a skittering crab, but they still gripped the keyboard like a set of wolverine claws. My fourth finger slowly began to relax its rigor mortis, but much of the time I still seemed to be pawing at the keyboard when I should have been delicately tapping. The 545 sonata was labeled, infuriatingly, "For beginners," and I began to see a hidden meaning in that phrase. What he meant wasn't so much that the skill level was for beginners, but that he had a Socratic *message* for beginners: "The one thing you must know is that you do not know."

As I left the biographies behind—Spitta, Schweitzer, Wolff, and the rest—there was still so much I didn't understand. Indeed, the mysteries of Bach seemed to make up a theme in their own right. And only some of them were due to the absence of evidence; the true enigmas reached beyond mere ignorance. Superficially, there were the puzzles Bach himself proposed, such as the Houdemann canon, whose cryptic runes are meant to be interpreted by a series of musical clues. A solution consists of a harmonically sound canon that observes some or all of these hints. Among them are the clefs to the left, each of which suggests a different starting tone (G, C, A, and D), and the upside down clefs to the right, which suggest inversion and another key signature. (Investigating Bach's mysteries tends to be a cross between math homework and religious revelation.) Why did he use this "enigmatic notation?" Why all the secrecy? Perhaps because music was only just transitioning from an alchemy, preserved within the guild and passed on from master to apprentice, to publicly verified science, propagated by scholars.[8] That is why his brother had locked the little orphan out of his library, thinking of music as a trade secret to be hoarded. The mystery of music was still reserved to the initiate, but with one foot in the enlightenment; soon bourgeois drawing rooms would be filled with instruments like in the paintings of Vermeer, along with piano-for-dummies manuals that laid everything bare. Or perhaps the puzzle canons reflect an essentially esoteric worldview, the product of a mystery religion. Or maybe puzzles are just fun, and his friend Houdemann enjoyed them. Eventually, dueling Mattheson, eager not to be outwitted by Bach, and many other musicians tried their hand, and many solutions turn out to be possible.

Another puzzle canon is connected to *The Goldberg Variations*, whose significance seems greater and greater the more one learns, despite its soporific intent. When they found Bach's own printed copy in the 1970s, there was appended a set of fourteen canons based on the *Goldberg* theme, written in Bach's own hand, which, when added to the presence of the theme in Anna Magdalena's notebook, suggests a genuine obsession. (It also suggests a certain slyness; in these canons the theme lies all naked and unadorned, making it even more conspicuous how cunningly he has disguised it in the variations, so that most listeners enjoy the piece merely out of affect or because they have been told they must, not because they are following along.) One of these canons is the sheet music represented in the famous and only verifiable portrait of Bach, which is extremely gratifying since it means *The Goldberg Variations* are inscribed within it. Another was also previously known, since he had dedicated a version of it to a theology student a few years before his death. At the bottom, Bach had written, *Symbolum: Christus Coronabit Crucigeros*, "Motto: Christ will Crown the Crossbearers." There is thus some connection between the puzzle canon and this Christian saying, which evidently spoke to him, as he was passed over for lesser men, watched his children die, and was tormented by the bureaucracy. But what is the connection to the canon?

As with all real mysteries, one can only speculate. Some see a chiasmus in the fully realized canons, as the regular and inverted melodies seem to form the X-shaped letter *chi* in Greek; some see a reference to the stigmata of Christ in a five-note descending sequence. [9] And in fact, Bach often used the letter *chi* to stand for "Christ" and for "cross" in his manuscripts. Moreover, there is Bach's monogram to consider, which he used as his personal seal and incorporated into stemware, furniture, and who knows what else. The letters *JSB* are written right-side up, diagonally from left to right, and in inversion from right to left in the back, as well. (Connoisseurs will recognize that there were in fact many versions of the seal differing in detail; our representation captures the important features.) The crossing *S*'s produce an *X*-shaped *chi*, so that Bach is bearing the cross, and in doing so he is crowned.

It may be that all of this is just fanciful, and devotees do sometimes torture Bach's numbers into false confession.

Cabalistic fallacies abound—some claim there are fourteen *Goldberg* canons because the numbers corresponding to B, A, C, and H in the alphabet add up to fourteen, and there is much more of the same. But it *is* curious: the monogram is attested in the 1720s, making it too early to associate with any genuinely royal titles. Perhaps Bach thought that having worked for a princeling or a duke merited a crown, or perhaps he just ran around telling people, "I'm the king of music!" but that isn't consistent with the picture one gets of Bach, proud but not boastful. So perhaps Bach really did encode in his music and monogram elaborate references to the cross he bore and the crown he hoped to wear.

Nearly all of the major works contain similar mysteries. The *Musical Offering* was offered to King Frederick the Great after he humiliated Bach by demanding impossible feats of counterpoint, but was the humiliation intentional as some have alleged? And was Carl Philipp Emanuel Bach, who worked for the King, in on it? More importantly, how is a "well-tempered" instrument to be tuned? The point of *The Well-Tempered Clavier* is that by tuning appropriately you can modulate across all of the keys, as long as you accept some impurities. But we can't help wondering precisely how Bach did temper his clavier *well*, and he doesn't say. (The early biographer Forkel says that he could tune his harpsichord with amazing swiftness, but neglects to mention how.) Here, again, there are those who turn to esoteric solutions. The original cover page, for instance, contains a series of decorative curlicues which have been interpreted to hold the secret. You simply flip the page upside down, note that the *C* in *Clavier* abuts a curlicue which is therefore the note C, temper in fifths according to the convolutions in the curlicues . . . assume the lotus position and light the incense. (And yet music tuned this way really does end up being quite beautiful, *almost* to the point that one might suffer the harpsichord.)[10]

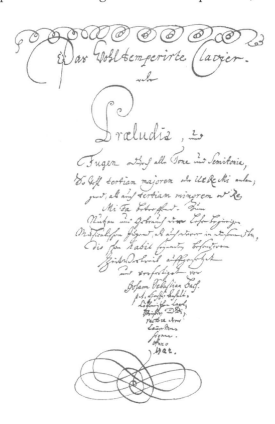

The point of *The Art of Fugue*, in turn, is the massive quadruple fugue intended to cap off and summarize all that he had learned about the craft of fugue-writing—and yet the work seems incomplete. We are left with a giant anti-climax, as we hear B-A-C-H, only for the composer to die at the score, at least according to what someone—perhaps Carl Philipp Emanuel—has scribbled into the autograph manuscript. But on one theory Bach already *had* finished the manuscript in a now lost fragment that was to be integrated later.[11] And there even exist heretical counter-theories according to which the unfinished piece was never intended for the *Art of Fugue* at all.[12]

This mystery, too, will never be fully resolved, given the inscrutable mess of evidence, of fragments, letters, Post-it Notes, watermarks, ink-types, the P 200 manuscript, the crucial *Beilage* no. 3, the handwriting analysis, and all the rest that ultimately remains ambiguous. But there is also something sublime in the way things turned out. Ending on B-A-C-H is of course droll, but what is more significant is the incompleteness itself. Conventionally-minded people resist a jarring end to it all. Carl went so far as to *truncate* the published work to avoid an ending quite so abrupt, without even indicating what he had done, and appended additional music to compensate the buyers. (The price was lowered from ten to five to four thalers, and sold thirty copies, including one for—who else?—Mattheson.) I have attended performances even now in which the pianist apologizes for this incompleteness and likewise proceeds to another work in order to avoid anticlimax, like a comedian who "improves" on his joke by prattling on after the punch line. But of course anyone with a soul will feel the mystic rightness of hearing the name intoned one last time, before the music lurches off the track unexpectedly, that final D hanging in the air as we continue the music in our heads by inertia for a few bars, until we reconcile ourselves to the crash and remember that the dream of the return is always in a way unfulfilled, at least if the journey has been worthwhile.

As I set down my books, I pictured Bach looking out his window to the west—*westwärts schweift der Blick*, as Wagner sings. I saw him looking past the city walls, at the silhouette of the Merseburg Cathedral in the distance, as the boys cried next door and the letters piled up next to the freshly ruled paper and the ink pots, and decided that Wagner was perhaps right after all, that Bach *was* a kind of sphinx with a wig as his headdress, standing at the portals of music to interrogate us, not straightforwardly like Mozart, but enigmatically, in accordance with the fundamental mysteries of music, and life, and ultimately of reality itself—why we should respond to patterns of sound as profoundly as we do, how polyphony and the impossible accord of independent melody should exist at all, how consciousness and the experience of music should arise from unconscious blocks of matter, and why we alone should be here to hear it (Bach's golden record on *Voyager* still unanswered), and all the way back around to whether we could tap out eight notes in a row in C major.

5

The Piano

I started out thinking of my piano as a bird with a raised black wing, but now it came to resemble a Venus flytrap. I dangled my torso over the strings dusting late at night, and imagined the lid snapping to, swallowing me whole. Christopher used to forecast my death by IKEA, noting my perilous bookcases, tottering full and unsecured, and I enjoyed the romance of it, of having an encounter with a copy of Plato or Parfit so intimate that the weight of their arguments cracked my skull. But now I read less and played more, and the death I imagined was cacophonous and sensuous; I would be ingested by my piano like an animal I'd imprudently domesticated, and then perhaps be strangled by the steel strings, or crushed by the twenty tons of pressure on the harp.

I had these thoughts in the evening, when the light changed and the keys no longer looked ivory but a bronzed beige against the Edison bulb. The soundproofing I had installed stilled the reverberations of the small room, and in the silence the world seemed to contract to C4, key and vertebra, as I laid into the first invention and felt a tingle at the nape of my neck. At times like these the music seemed once again to speak a natural language I could almost make out, muffled syllables in a foreign tongue, and I felt myself absorbing into the piano. The hammers seemed connected to my fingertips, like limbs I was trying to learn to use again after an accident, still externalized but reflexively familiar. At first I pictured this relation as quite simple: my finger depressed the key, the key was attached to some sort of pivot, and at the other end of the key was the hammer that struck the strings. Down went the finger, up went the hammer. But on reflection, this was quite impossible; there had to be more to it. If one simply pushed down a key with a hammer at the other end, then keeping the key depressed would keep the hammer against the string, which would prevent it from vibrating, and playing would require some bizarre form of marimba-like tapping that would rule out sustained tones. What is required is some mechanism to *fling* the hammer at the string and then let it fall back, but in such a way that it doesn't then rebound against the strings, or prevent rapidly repeated notes. Simultaneously, there must be some opposing mechanism to keep the strings quiet when they aren't struck, but which is disengaged by pressing a key. And most important of all is the feel. Depending on exactly which system is employed to accomplish all these aims, the keys will either feel squishy, or sticky, or like nothing at all. The feel of the action is everything, since this determines the extent to which the piano ultimately seems like an extension of your body.

Late at night, in bibulous curiosity, I removed my piano's action to see how it worked. I felt almost embarrassed removing all the shame-covering wood leaves—first the fallboard by jimmying and tugging a bit (did the wine vitiate consent?), next the cheek blocks, and finally the keyslip, leaving the action exposed, until it too slid out. I was astonished by the machinery that came into view. Beneath the soft curves of the casing lay an elaborate artifice of springs and levers. And yet the artifice itself had a certain organic quality to it, each unit repeated eighty-eight times like the segmentation of an insect, and made of wood that I watered weekly to control for humidity by the $300 contraption that hornswoggling salesman had palmed off on me.

I examined more closely this apparatus connecting player and string. Where once finger plucked at the lyre, or plectrum pecked at the harpsichord, an immense complication of wood, wire, and felt now intervened. Its central purpose was to solve the problem of playing soft and loud, *piano e forte*, which was impossible with the plectrum of the harpsichord, which either plucked or didn't. (Dynamics were indeed possible on the hammered clavichord, but this instrument was a stunted toy that was more or less inaudible.) Bartolomeo Cristofori had the flash of insight around 1700, when Bach was still a teenager in Lüneburg, and the outlines of his idea have been retained. The key pivots around a balance rail and pushes up the damper from the strings at the far end. Meanwhile, three or four fifths down the key, another raised point pushes up a shoe-shaped assembly with a jack at the end. As the jack rises, it rubs against a soft pea-shaped organ, the clitoris of the piano, which sends the hammer to which it's attached shooting up toward the string, where it strikes for $\frac{1}{250}$ of a second before rebounding downward, while the hermaphrodite piano cries out in ecstasy.

The real genius, though, lies in what comes next, tracing back to Sébastien Érard's double escapement mechanism of 1821. As the jack moves upward across the pea, it allows the hammer to escape from the strings. Meanwhile, a lever has been raised to catch the hammer to prevent it from falling all the way down again. This keeps it close to the string, which allows for rapid repeated notes. But if the key is fully released, the hammer escapes to its fully inactive position, and the damper settles upon the string to silence it. Through it all, by the labors of Cristofori, Silbermann, Érard, and many others, the finger feels intimately connected to the strings, despite all of these intervening complications, a triumph of iterated craftsmanship.

From another point of view, the action of the piano is literally a machine, in the sense used in physics. The point is to manipulate the direction and magnitude of the force applied to the keys. When we strip away all the complications, the mechanism is essentially a compound lever; the whole design functions first to produce a relatively massive force, which is then harnessed for a frenetic result at the other end, like a trebuchet. (One pictures Cristofori reading Galileo's treatise on mechanics in his workshop amid all the sawdust and music.) First the key rotates around a fulcrum, yielding a mechanical advantage that multiplies the force we put in, just like a crowbar. But the key connects up with the hammer by another fulcrum, this time arranged like a broom, which multiplies not the force but the speed of the stick (or hammer).

I carefully reinserted the action, pleased to have done only moderate damage—a couple of scratches and a few missing pieces, no more—and contemplated the instrument as a whole. The piano is essentially a harp laid on its side, and there is something moving about the deep connection between a modern piano and the ancient lyre. The main differences are that the piano is a percussive instrument in which the strings are hammered rather than plucked, and the introduction of the iron frame in the nineteenth century, which made it possible to greatly increase the number and thickness of the strings, resulting in a louder, richer instrument covering seven octaves. Sometimes the percussive qualities of the piano can be exploited, as in the hammered dulcimer effect in Bach's Prelude in F Minor in Book II of *The Well-Tempered Clavier*, but as often musicians agonize to conceal these qualities, like Debussy, who somehow managed to turn the piano into a billowy confection of drapes waving lazily in the breeze at some villa, or Ravel, who turned it into games of water. On the whole, the piano is the most logically organized instrument, since the keys just represent the notes of this harp in ascending order, and they are perfectly easy to strike. Every other instrument, by contrast, has some stupid and illogical feature, some weird protuberance that must be squeezed or fondled awkwardly, or else it is hopelessly obscure how to play the desired note, since it involves pursing your lips correctly or spitting at the instrument in the right way, or because the tuning of the strings makes the relationship between adjacent notes more or less random. The instruments of the orchestra might as well be floofloovers and whohoopers for all the sense they make. The piano, by contrast, is perfectly straightforward. To the extent that it is difficult to play well, that is because the music is difficult and the human player flawed, not because the instrument was designed by Dr. Seuss.

The process of my piano digesting its human began with small things. I went through half a dozen pans left boiling while I went off to practice just a phrase or two, only to discover a heap of smoldering teflon an hour later. My clothes all shrank in the dryer, the bathroom filled with steam. Then I started putting off returning calls and missing appointments, and I complained to Lauren about long trips away which meant I couldn't practice. I sold my camera gear since I no longer saw any point in other hobbies; I wrote two books with my left hand and some infuriating dictation software. More grandiosely, I began to wonder what I had done all those useless years without my piano, the way lovers come to regret all the time they lost without each other. I felt an intense jealousy. It drove me mad to think that this very instrument had suffered the inept caresses of some lothario before I arrived on the scene.

You would think I was a virtuoso, and yet all this merely prevented me from being even worse—I still couldn't play Mozart correctly, even as I began experimenting with the more approachable parts of *The Well-Tempered Clavier.* You might similarly suppose that I was playing with or at least in front of others, and deriving some social benefit from the piano, but that wasn't the case, either. The piano was a black coffin to climb inside and hide, padded and still, like the album art for Iron Maiden's *Piece of Mind.* Once I kept playing when Lauren came home, and I could hear her silence as I continued awhile, and when I went out to investigate, there she was, softly weeping. After that, I no longer played in her presence, and I carefully dropped the fallboard whenever I heard the car pull up. Performing in front of other musicians, in turn, made me anxious lest they should wrinkle their noses at me, while guests who were unmusical and praised me to the skies I hated all the more for their baseless enjoyment. (The exception was Christopher, whose criticism was so inevitable and yet delicate that it hardly seemed threatening.)

I looked up from the keys. Perhaps studying the piano was ultimately a way of avoiding other people, or more subtly, a way of justifying avoiding other people. Lauren pointed out that I treated humanity in general as an obstacle course to surmount and evade, which stung with truth, though I mostly blamed the Internet, which had made avoiding people ever easier, as we devolved into a society of lonely masturbators, and which made you actually *want* to see people less and less as you observed what they were really like on the Web, as if it had been invented to turn us all into jaded misanthropes. Technology enabled us to say anything, when it was often a tragedy that we could talk to one another at all.

The shiny black reflected back my hands, and I began to conceive of all of my relationships in musical terms. Lauren was the overture to *The Magic Flute*, a flutter of eighth notes alla breve, all joy in E-flat major except for the occasional modulation into the minor; Father was "Semper Fidelis"; personal conflict was an unresolved suspension in which the harmony changed but one of the notes failed to keep up and grated; the administration was a series of diminished chords; the dean's speech about the humanities was a deceptive cadence; my students banged their anvils in 9/8 time; Shivani's senior thesis on the paradox of tragedy was a brilliant turn through the circle of fifths; the memory of Mother, of visiting Selby Gardens together just before the end, of her painted eyebrows and headscarf, smiling amid the orchids, was a *Tristan* chord, ambiguous and difficult to interpret. Each encounter in the day was another beat, another accord or dissonance to prepare for and leave behind by stepwise contrary motion, until at last we came to the cadential 6/4 chord, the V chord, and finally all the dissonances resolved into the gin and tonic, and I was alone again.

In another direction lay the positive attractions of the piano. In some ways it was addictive and drug-like, as when I was learning new music and felt the compulsion of solving the puzzle by inserting one last piece, and I kept going over and over the last few bars in order to finish, or when I could see the next level up nearly accessible, and I craved the feeling of *Success!* in mastering that stage of the game. Or sometimes the addiction felt more like drugs that work by rendering other experiences less significant by comparison, as everything else gets reranked into fours and fives compared to the new nine, as when leaving the piano in the morning to trudge off to work and chew at the bit. But at a deeper level, instruments come to function as prosthetics or artificial organs that address deficits we never knew we had. The piano was a machine that allowed me to summon and inspect the impressions of the fading day, or my fears for the next, or even the nightmares of the past, the distant voices of people mumbling over one another while I lay awake at night. Each would come marching past my music desk as I worked on my inventions, waiting to be processed or palliated, the cast of my subconscious circling hand in hand like in Fellini. Musicians can no more live without their instruments than polio victims can survive without their ventilators.

But before long it was time to trundle off. At work we needed to discuss the upcoming cuts in our funding and the president's Thriving Workplace Initiative, which promised to boost morale through a series of interminable meetings. Back in my office, a lacrosse player brought a note excusing her from half of all my classes so she could travel with the team, while another insisted that a B+ contravened his human rights. An older gentleman came by and introduced himself as a local transcendental humanist; he produced a business card that read, "I think, therefore I am/I feel, therefore I care/I dream, therefore I reach." I gently explained that my surly colleagues were unlikely to be of use to him, and he stormed out in a rage. I graded a paper on The Apology that ended with the sentence, "I believe u should fight for what u believe in at all cost." Finally, I staggered home to my piano and played Philip Glass—Cylon baseship music, as Lauren called it. All this had happened before, all this would happen again. I longed to be a hybrid of man and machine, to recite mystical snippets from my students' papers, which sometimes sounded like gibberish but in fact expressed the will of God.

To understand Bach and the piano one must to some extent understand the organ. Bach was a keyboard player, but with no real loyalty to any one instrument. There was the harpsichord, the clavichord, and even a primitive version of the piano toward the end of his life. But he spent much of his professional career at the organ, and in some respects it is the organ that defines him—certainly many of his contemporaries would have seen it that way. Since people nowadays rarely get to hear the organ and don't have much appreciation for Bach's organ output, a great deal of his best and most characteristic work lies neglected, setting aside the Toccata and Fugue in D Minor from his juvenilia. Mostly we think of the organ as a spooky Halloween sonority, or else a boring church contraption, and so the music suffers from our associations with Count Dracula and the hymnal.

The idea behind the organ is to set off vibrating columns of air in the pipes rather than plucking or hammering strings. Since the pipes have fixed dimensions, organs require one pipe for each pitch or key on the manual. This already gives rise to considerable complications, since in

Bach's day each key had to be mechanically connected to the pipes, which were often situated at a distance, so that an ingenious system of stickers and trackers and roller-boards were required to transmit the downward motion of the key vertically and horizontally, sometimes around corners, often underneath the player's seat, to the tone valve beneath the pipe. But of course a varied sound presupposes not just one pipe per key, but a vast array of *ranks* of pipes in different timbres, some of which sounded more like flutes or strings or reeds than pipes (apart from the true-blue diapasons), and which could be variously combined, so that a single key activated many pipes making the same note but often at different octaves, and sometimes even "mutations" in a harmonizing pitch for a richer sound. In order to control these varying ranks, there were dozens of "stops" that could be pulled out at the console in order to shift thin wooden sliders at the base of the pipes, each drilled with holes that would align or misalign with the pipe entrances to pass or stop the air. The sliders criss-crossed the channels opened by the tone valves, so a pipe would only sound when its key was pressed and its slider unstopped.

The arrangement of pipes that emerged in the Baroque has been described in terms of a *Werkprinzip*, according to which the organ was really several sub-organs, each with its own distinctive mix of sounds, each controlled by its own manual, and each visually identifiable as a separate unit. Thus, the main *Hauptwerk* was located centrally above the console (sometimes topped with an *Oberwerk*), below it was a *Brustwerk*, and behind the player, shielding him from his audience and directing any flatulence he might experience in their direction, was the little *Rückpositiv*. And in addition to the manuals, there were usually pedals, which the player was expected to control as nimbly as the keys—in Bach the pedal part routinely calls for intricate sixteenth note runs by foot. The pedals were connected to huge pipes organized into column formations that flanked the other divisions like a hulking dragon's retracted wings. The largest of these were thirty-two feet tall and could play down to 16 Hz or four octaves below middle C, though few organs did so cleanly, since 16 cycles per second is a frequency very difficult to render coherent. This made the organ the only instrument to traverse the full range of human hearing, 16 Hz to 16,000 Hz, which in turn makes other instruments seem incomplete and disappointing by comparison. And feeding all of these pipes were the bellows, which the poor interns had to operate by foot, with the aid of a lever, so as to pump air into the reservoir, which maintained even pressure for the instrument through a series of inflatable bladders and release valves.

The many ranks of pipes allowed for tremendous variety in registration and tone-color. They also made it possible to adjust dynamics. Pressing an organ key harder doesn't make things louder, since however hard you press you still only open a valve. But some stops were louder than others and of course more or fewer of them could be opened, allowing for a very different kind of dynamic performance from hammered instruments like the piano. And when required, all of those tubes could make a great deal of sound indeed. We think of Baroque music as relatively "light," comparing 18th-century church or chamber music to the orchestras of Beethoven or Wagner. But it is entirely the other way around: the triple fortes of Beethoven are pig-squeals next to what a thousand organ pipes can put out. (In fact, in his noisier passages one sometimes suspects that Beethoven is trying to recapture the organs he played when he was young.) The organ is heavy metal before there was such a thing.

All of this can be illustrated in the monumental Passacaglia in C Minor BWV 582, which features a repeating ostinato theme with twenty variations overlaid. The theme slithers through the depths of the pedals, then gradually builds to a cataclysm sure to frighten small children, as the pipes hit us with that lower-than-low C and thirty-two feet of vibrating air. The piece contains five key moments which the performer must observe and try to mark out through a combination of registration and performance technique: the entrance of the first variation after we have heard the eight bars of the theme; the flip that marks the second half of the piece in the eleventh variation, where Bach suddenly shifts the theme from the bass into the soprano; the first climax at the twelfth variation; the disappearance of the pedal and gradual thinning out until there is no counterpoint at all, just a single voice rising over and over again in the fifteenth variation; and then the triumphant return of the theme in the bass accompanied by massive chords in the second climax at the sixteenth variation, which takes us home to the conclusion.

Organists find different ways of screwing all this up. I had begun attending organ performances, but it was difficult to find 18th-century tracker organs in the local strip malls and megachurches, and so I felt compelled to try recordings, and I bought a pair of six-foot-panel loud-speakers that resembled the monolith in *2001* along with a subwoofer to do them some justice. But finding the perfect 582 recording proved elusive. Some performers took the approach of starting out soft and then building steadily to the first climax, but this meant that the first variation made its entrance rather meekly, a mush of somnolent flutes, when it was clear that Bach intended not just to enter but to *make an entrance*. Others came in hard, but didn't allow for rising drama at the first climax, or they ignored the climax altogether. (The correct approach was to start off brassy and bold, and then dial things back around the sixth variation, whose thinner texture calls for restraint, allowing things to build back up.) Still others failed to mark the flip, or the disappearance of the pedal and the solo voice, which skilled organists can endow with a magical, shimmering quality, especially on, say, the 1714 Silbermann organ at Freiberg, whose *Brustwerk* has the tone of its eponymous maker.

The organ was among the most complicated machines that had ever been devised, and its sibilant creators (Scherer, Schnitger, Silbermann) were consummate *Fachleute* responsible for all aspects of manufacture, nearly everything being made on-site. A large organ contained several dozen ranks and thousands of pipes, each of which required meticulous care in construction, voicing, and tuning, and each had to be connected mechanically to the console, which might itself have four manuals, each assigned to a different division of pipes, pre-configurable with a sound suited to the performance by arranging the stops, or else more interns would have to assist with adjusting the stops on the fly. And all of this was at the finger- and toe-tips of tiny Bach, whom I pictured far below in a crane shot from above the pedal works, a long shadow cast by the hall light as he entered from the side, dwarfed by this colossus which enabled him to fill a church with sound worthy of it, music on a scale entirely out of proportion with the human frame but commensurate with his vision of God. The stained windows had once enlightened the cathedrals by a feat of engineering and an act of devotion; now the ranks of pipes filled the reformation churches with music, the *verbum Dei* to the fiat lux of the clerestory. Settling into the cockpit, Bach lay encased in his biomechanical suit like the pilot in *Alien*, connected by wood and wire to the thousands of pipes, a hybrid of metal and leather and human, and as he spun into action, shifting from manual to manual to engage now the flutes, now the trombones or a mixture, adjusting the sound minutely to match the character of the music, whether it was to bring out the delicacy in a solo passage or to engage a giant chorus toward the end, while his knees bobbed up and down and swiveled on his hips across the pedals, and a throng of bellow-boys and assistants pedaled and huffed, all to project his system of mad counterpoint into the very bowels of the parishioners, he represented the summit of what his civilization could accomplish, their pyramids, their Saturn V rocket. (The effect of all this on the audience? They filed complaints against Bach with the bureaucracy for playing too long and loud, which is as if Americans had filed complaints against the moon landing. No wonder he wanted a *Rückpositiv*.)

The tragedy of it, though, is that Bach never got to have a truly great organ of his own—those in Leipzig were mediocre in the scheme of things. But he did come close. Bach's first wife, Maria, died in the summer of 1720. A few months later, the organist at the St. Jacobi church in Hamburg died as well, opening up a position that would inherit one of the finest organs in the world, the 1693 Schnitger, with its five divisions. One of its few rivals, as it happened, was likewise in Hamburg, at St. Catherine's, presided over by the great northern master Johann Adam Reincken, a man Bach had venerated and journeyed to hear in his youth. At ninety-seven, he was the grand old man of the organ ever since Buxtehude had passed away. Bach went to visit Hamburg in the fall and was invited to play at St. Catherine's, in front of Reincken and all of the leading figures of the city, Germany's largest at the time. Reincken was not only one of the greatest living organists, but he was on the judging panel for the St. Jacobi position—the performance at St. Catherine's was in effect an audition. And if these weren't high enough stakes, Reincken was notoriously prickly and vain. When word had gotten out that he intended to replace his own predecessor at St. Catherine's, another virtuoso, someone had wondered who could be so rash, and Reincken sent the skeptic a copy of his signature work, a chorale on "By the Rivers of Babylon," so that he might judge for himself how "rash" he was. (As if to confirm its importance, Bach later copied out this piece in cramped tablature at the age of fifteen.) On his title pages Reincken referred to himself as *celebratissimus*—the superlative, not the comparative—and dueling Mattheson tells us that he was "a constant admirer of the fair sex, and much addicted to the wine cellar of the council."[1]

All of these things must have been in Bach's mind as he ascended into the aerie. He knew that this was probably the greatest organ in the world, and afterward proclaimed that it, almost alone, could produce a perfectly clear low C on the thirty-two-foot pipes. He would have ascertained that the organ was tuned in meantone—not in well-temperament—so that he had to exercise care in his modulations to avoid the dissonant "wolf" interval, and made some last-minute adjustments in the registration. Behind him were all the great men of the city, the committee that would decide on his appointment, prickly Reincken, his childhood idol, and dozens of distinguished musicians. And then Bach threw himself into a half hour improvisation on the "Rivers of Babylon," Reincken's personal showcase that Bach had copied those many years before. One imagines gasps in the audience and knowing looks—who was this upstart? And for thirty minutes! It was the ultimate statement of self-assurance, of the intention to take up Reincken's scepter, or perhaps pry it from his fist.

He kept on playing, on, and on, and on. An hour passed, then an hour and a half. Alien worlds ricocheted off the piers, sometimes too worked out to be genuinely improvisatory, and yet too irregular and well-connected throughout to be a series of fixed compositions. Always Bach watched his ground, never straying too close to forbidden realms like A-flat, where the wolf lurked in wait. This was before Liszt had invented the solo piano recital; virtuosity was still a novelty, as was the idea that it might be worth spending several hours listening to just one man. The organist was still half *Fachmann*, certainly not an Artist, and no one saw Bach as a composer to revere. And yet here was this man from the backwaters of Saxony doing things unattempted yet in that spaceship behind the *Rückpositiv*, things that hardly seemed possible. At last it was time for the finale, as the second hour drew to a close. It was surely here that Bach introduced what became a sensation—perhaps the greatest fugue of them all, BWV 542 in G minor, along with its fantasia. Years later people still remembered the subject of the fugue and its performance that day, the stunning complexity of its pedal lines that pushed the lungs of the organ to their limits, its allusions to Dutch music in honor of Reincken.

Filling the church with those dissonant chords toward the end, Bach must have thought of Maria and the horror of her death while he had been away traveling. If only he'd been there to save her somehow! And perhaps the reverberations outside St. Catherine's helped prepare the city for its own horror that was to come, when all this would burn in Operation Gomorrah, when the city would become a whirlwind of fire, and the asphalt would melt and stick to the children's feet as they ran, and people would watch their neighbors get sucked up into the giant vortex of fire that rose a thousand feet in the air, like a scene from Bosch, as if all the medieval visions of hell and the apocalypse had suddenly come true, wrecking all these churches and their precious organs, apart from those pipes carefully hidden away, or beaten into rifles in World War I. All this, somehow, seems now contained in BWV 542, the anthem of Hamburg and of German innocence and ingenuity that nevertheless augurs the darkness, the swastikas and the Lancasters. And yet Bach couldn't believe the darkness would prevail. There was music, there was life. He would remarry eventually. Perhaps someday he would be ready to talk to that pretty singer he had met in Cöthen. He had been unable to bring himself to end the fantasia in the major, as was customary, landing instead on a brutal G minor, but as he came to the end of the fugue he played the *tierce picarde*, the major-chord conclusion to a minor-key piece, the final affirmation of hope and of life. The bass seemed to echo an eternity after he lifted his fingers from the keyboard, but at last there was silence.

As Bach descended from the organ loft, his face surely illuminated like that of Moses descending Mount Sinai, he could see that there was some justice in the world. He had succeeded in realizing his own potential as a musician and in conveying all that he was capable of to an audience that could actually comprehend his art. There would be no complaints filed here. Crusty old Reincken, the curmudgeon, the tippler, greeted Bach and said to him simply, "I thought this art was dead, but I perceive that it still lives in you." It was an expression of the utmost arrogance in one sense, proclaiming all the other musicians around them worthless, and yet in the end Reincken expressed the humility of one who had thought himself the savior but finally realized he was only the baptist. Two years later he died and was buried, as he requested, with Buxtehude in Lübeck (*nunc dimittis, Domine, nunc dimittis*).

The musical community was in raptures. They were in a position to install a master in one of their own churches before anyone else was in a position to launch a bidding war. Not only was Reincken on the judging panel, but the search committee was led by the pastor at St. Jacobi, Erdmann Neumeister, who had written the libretti to several of Bach's cantatas. Everything seemed to align. The committee minutes state that Bach and several other candidates had come forward. Bach had to return home before the official trials at St. Jacobi, but this seems to have been waived in his case. After the auditions took place the committee delayed voting until they received a letter from Bach that has not survived. The minutes record that this letter was read aloud to all, but without describing its contents. They then proceeded to vote—not for Bach but for some nobody, an unskilled journeyman. Bach would not get his organ; he would bear a cross instead of a crown. All this had happened before and all this would happen again. It was just as when he'd been passed over for that son of the Kapellmeister at Weimar a few years earlier, and just as it would be again when he came in third for the job at Leipzig. Handel was the same age as Bach, but he was getting rich and famous in London with his operas. He had just performed for King George I a few months ago and women had *fainted*; money was pouring in; the South Sea Bubble burst, but Handel just skated away, charmed as Bach was blighted.

What could Bach's letter have said? How could the committee have voted against him despite what must have been Reincken and Neumeister's influence? Perhaps Bach withdrew, preferring to stay in Cöthen. Had he been denied permission to depart, or did he already have his eye on Anna? In seeking to understand all this, I thought about the search committees I had served on, and suddenly I wasn't so surprised. In academia, such committees begin with directives from the dean's office reflecting whatever political imperatives happen to be in vogue at the time, which must be carefully concealed in the official job notice because of their dubious legal standing; next, the faculty members bicker about what sort of person to hire, each seeking to shape the department in their own image, at whatever cost to the whole; whereupon the committee meets, and the members take turns subtly undermining one another in order to advance some favorite as a vehicle of their own ambitions; and finally, in the decisive meeting, when it appears that all is clear and in the open, you are outmaneuvered when someone sweeps in at the last second and raises a devastating objection to the obvious candidate—an objection that could be quite easily answered with a bit more time and a few emails to clear up some trivial misunderstandings, except that the éminence grise has waited until the last fifteen minutes of the meeting, and immediately moves for a vote which he wins. Perhaps, then, Neumeister lacked guile.

But in fact it is quite clear what happened. For shortly after the new organist was installed, Neumeister gave a sermon on the music of the angels at the birth of Christ, and closed with the observation—recorded by the ubiquitous Mattheson—that even if one of the angels of Bethlehem should come down from heaven and offer to become the organist at St. Jacobi, he would have to fly away empty-handed unless he came bearing *money*. And indeed, the earlier committee minutes reveal the following deliberations:

> There were many reasons not to introduce the sale of an organist's post, because it was part of the ministry of God; accordingly the choice should be free, and the capacity of the candidates should be more considered than the money. But if, after the selection had been made, the chosen candidate of his own free will wished to give a token of his gratitude, the latter could be accepted for the benefit of the church . . .[2]

I knew from experience what this meant. There had been two opposing parties, one that rejected pay-to-play—the harlotry of Babylon—and the simoniacs in favor. Since the organist hired was the son of a well-to-do citizen, there was more at stake than just the immediate payment, and many posts in the city were already for sale. Who knows what the finances of the church were like? Then a compromise was offered by someone in league with the simoniacs, who suggested that *of course* merit was the important thing, but it could hardly hurt to express a *willingness* to receive a *voluntary* donation after the fact! One that might help support, for example, critical renovations. And sure enough, the winner later expressed his gratitude by making a *four thousand–mark* donation to the church—a huge sum amounting to several times a decent salary.[3]

(Whether by coincidence or not, the organ at St. Jacobi was said to contain four thousand pipes, a very curious detail.) So either Bach wrote that he was willing to accept the post but was voted down anyway, or else he withdrew in disdain once he found out about these expectations. For Neumeister would hardly have excoriated his own congregation if Bach had withdrawn on other grounds and the best man won.

By the rivers of Hamburg we knelt down and wept.

I returned to the piano humbled by the organ. I almost pitied the instrument for its puny seven-octave range, the lack of sustain, its stunted proportions. But then I opened up the lid again, which I'd kept closed a while for a softer, muffled tone, and I was seduced by the ecstasy of all that gold, gazing on those coiled strings that waited to consume me. At night, the interior glowed against the black casing and the blue rug like gold at the bottom of the Rhine, which drove men mad when they thought they could take it from those incompetent nixies, or like the face of Vincent Vega opening the briefcase in *Pulp Fiction*. There it was, the metal heart of the thing.

The meaning of the piano as prosthetic had intensified over the years, especially in relation to teaching. Bookworms run off to grad school foolishly imagining they are preparing for a life of introverted seclusion, the life of the mind, when the best case scenario means becoming a teacher, who is by definition a public speaker, which is in turn the very nightmare of the bookworm. Plato, when he invented the university, posted a sign—"Let no one enter who doesn't know geometry," but it should have said "Let no one enter who doesn't wish to speak in front of hundreds of people for a living." Each morning I paused a moment at the lectern to collect myself, and gazed out at the drowsy faces expecting me to strike up, and thought of bolting out the door never to return, fearing I might forget what I was supposed to say. Sometimes these moments of dread would extend themselves, feed on themselves, as I began lecturing, until I started to stutter and had to cough in order to seem coherent. The only thing that helped in such moments was music, quietly singing to myself some line from Mozart or Bach, which bridged the gap between their boredom and my fear, which were mixed together like in the trenches of Verdun.

My stupid lectures felt fake the way the *Brandenburg Concertos* were fake—if I listened carefully I could hear recorders twittering in the back. I yearned to talk to people simply, face-to-face in conversation, like Socrates or like Bach's confessions at the keyboard. To prepare, instead of rushing off to school each day, I sat at the piano early in the morning and meditated on all that was to come, and I found a measure of relief in finding a theme I could sing to myself, a kind of incantation to recite. To be a teacher is to be boring; school itself renders your subject dull to a certain degree, no matter how enthusiastic *you* are about it, and it is a terrible fate to bore people for a living.

The piano could even temper the past, I found, summoning the dead and the forgotten as if by libations of milk and honey. There was Christopher threatening to kick in my kneecaps during Mr. Witura's algebra class, asking me if I was familiar with "Seek and Destroy," there was the dingy hallway where I ate lunch in structural silence (the bruised fruit, the styrofoam, the never-ending John Hughes movie) and there was Lauren and her apotropaic leg, still far off, somewhere in New York or California, unable to make me human yet. I questioned each shade as it appeared, and found some peace in this as well, assigning to each its appropriate chord.

Throughout this time I naturally sought out a great many recordings of Bach on the piano, sometimes just to listen, sometimes to understand better how to play. Finding a canonical recording of each work that mattered to me became a fixation, but there were many obstacles to overcome. It began with the quality of the recording itself, the sound of the piano that was utilized, how it was miked, and the engineering behind the production, all of which typically resulted in a thick, swampy sound, when what was required was a thin reed that could slice through all that counterpoint—not the dreaded harpsichord, but something *just* this side of the piano. Glenn Gould's Steinway had that gutted quality, but few other pianos did, and not everyone could afford to retain a technician as Gould did to sit around fiddling with the instrument to keep it in shape. But even if you had the right piano on hand, there was the question of recording quality, and everyone knows that the better the performance the worse the recording, an iron law of audiophilia designed to punish those who harbor a dark passion for sound quality. You can actually find Albert Schweitzer playing Bach on the organ, but only through a wind tunnel in the distance; the best recordings of Wagner were made live for Italian radio in the 1950s, and they aren't even in stereo. Likewise, Gould's recordings are pretty poor, since many of them are either older, or else from the disastrous days of early digital. András Schiff performed my canonical version of *The Art of Fugue*, but the engineering and the piano itself conspired to produce what my Magnepan speakers faithfully transmitted as a muffled thud.

Of course, what really mattered was the playing itself. Bach requires virtuosity, but not in the way that the more obviously crowd-whoring repertoire does—the chestnuts of Chopin, Liszt, and the rest—and thus much of the talent pool doesn't bother with Bach. Many of the virtuosos of China, for instance, don't seem interested, though I was fascinated by Xiao-Mei Zhu, who studied Bach on a forbidden piano in a Chinese labor camp, sometimes whilst in a refrigerator, which physically modeled my own desperation that resulted from constraints that were both greater and infinitely less than hers. Zhu's *Goldbergs* were my recording of choice for a while, or at least they were stiff competition to Nikolayeva, the babushka who preceded her in my affections. Others clearly didn't have much of a taste for Bach, but made one or two tantalizing forays that were just enough to drive you mad with what might have been, as with Martha Argerich, whose Toccata in C Minor sounded even more gutted than Gould's version, and whose performance was every bit as virile and commanding, or Ivo Pogorelić, whose technique was almost beyond belief—but none of that mattered since they decided to throw their lives away and focus on the Romantics. Still others did condescend to play Bach, but were unable or unwilling to produce the right sort of virtuosity, which requires sounding as close to a machine as possible, with fanatical regularity and precision, which in turn has to be organically modulated in certain situations, as when playing a loose toccata or prelude. Tureck and Angela Hewitt, for example, played rather slow and carefully, and those whip-and-tingle numbers from *The Well-Tempered Clavier*, or some of *The Goldberg Variations*, failed to catch fire as a result, and in the end the impression was one of a very talented schoolgirl playing for her relatives. On the other hand, there were those like Murray Perahia or Richter, who were perhaps too good for their own good, and smoothed out every last crease and wrinkle by their constant legato and refinement, even when a certain rusticity was called for. These pianists never sounded bad, just a bit overdressed; they wore top hats and evening gowns even as they sang of cabbages.

And then there was Gould, mad Glenn Gould in his weird little chair. His taste was perfect—he hated all the right things—and for a while he had the perfect piano, until they dropped his poor Steinway CD 318 off a truck and broke its back (just as they had done previously to number 174), and instead of having the good sense to take it out back and shoot it, he tried to nurse the thing back to health, which only prolonged the agony.[4] And Gould was formidable away from the piano. One sees this in his jokey compositions ("So You Want to Write a Fugue?") and in the many lectures and radio dramas, especially *The Quiet in the Land*. At his best, no one in the world was better, or had more of the right kind of talent. His secret was to play an inelegant staccato, to tap at the keys in a way that emphasized the mechanical properties of the music, contrary to the advice of every piano teacher ever, and to break up each moment in time like stop-motion animation or a pulsing strobe light, but to do so with such virtuosity that the final effect was to etch each line of the polyphony into your consciousness with a surreal clarity that made you think you had never really heard this music before.

But Gould wasn't really interested in *playing* music, and not just in the sense that he quit the stage. By his own admission he was a theorist at heart, who investigated his subject by way of critical interpretations, advancing theses that sometimes belonged in conferences or journal articles, but instead found their way onto recordings. When these succeeded, he performed a service closer to archaeology than music, by exhuming ideas and scores long dead. ("People see *The Goldberg Variations* as a museum piece that no one really wants to hear," one imagines him saying, "but if you play it fast, fun and casual it's a ripping good time!") There were many works I would never have understood, whose greatness would have eluded me entirely, but for Gould unearthing them. But often his underlying thesis was so bizarre that the recording itself drove you crazy, and eventually you just got tired of the humming and the groaning, his face hovering close over the keyboard, of the imaginary injuries, his lawsuits over being clapped on the shoulder, and of all his magnificent bullshit. He was a mad scientist who sometimes produced fusion and sometimes blew up the house.

The main drawback to being self-taught is that you have no one to blame for your incompetence; the advantage is that you are forced not just to learn, but to learn how to learn. Of course, looking back, Christopher had been my teacher all along, as all true friends are teachers and good teaching is a kind of friendship. In a way, it was a psychological crutch to pretend he wasn't. I mostly managed to discover only what he had told me about long ago, and often returned to him his own counsels with Emerson's sense of "alienated majesty." Part of the horror of industrial-scale teaching was precisely the absence of friendship, and even on a smaller scale, the bureaucracy made such things impossible, as students came to class to fulfill obscure administrative requirements, or because all the classes with "sex" in the title had already filled. And those who abused their students, and then those seeking to correct those abuses by trials and tribunals, produced a coldness that deterred improprieties and friendship alike. But I thought, too, of the brilliant students I'd had—Shivani was applying to grad school now—and took comfort that not even schools and their administrators could entirely root out the spirit of inquiry and joy of learning.

Artistic progress is like Augustine's theory of evil, privative, mostly a matter of achieving insight into what is dark, the opposite of what the theory of unconscious genius would suggest. A good teacher can help you with all this initially (though more likely he will just yell at you to practice more and not to forget the metronome), but eventually students must learn to diagnose themselves, and a capacity for self-diagnosis isn't something anyone else can endow us with, any more than our holy men can make us holy, or our heroes can make us worthy of them. We expect the wrong thing of our teachers, that they transform us into what we wish to be, when all they really can do is suggest to us what we're capable of on our own, which is part of what Plato meant in saying that knowledge is remembrance of what is already latent. We want our teachers to be plastic surgeons when they are more like lenses and lighthouses.

I finally returned to Bach after nearly a year of Mozart. I was a bigamist returning from his second wife in Florida to his favorite up north. I didn't have much to show for it. I still couldn't play scales properly; my fingers refused to undulate softly like fronds of seaweed. And yet one fine morning in spring, somewhere toward the end of my third year, something was in the air.

I began sheepishly playing the subject, my old favorite, the C minor from *The Well-Tempered Clavier*, which I felt compelled to articulate without the short staccato notes the theme otherwise demands. Since the subject is supposed to be examined on all sides in the course of the piece, it really ought to be played consistently, but I had gotten it in my head that it deserved special, regal treatment at the outset as well as in its triumphant appearance at the end. The theme began by jerking you up and down in a *V*-shaped motion punctuated by two short notes and then added heft with two heavy beats, but I mashed down the keys heavily throughout for emphasis.

So far so good: I had made it past the first couple of measures, but I usually floundered right around here, as the bass gave its version of the theme, completing the exposition. There was a false subject-entry that I always fell for, even though I knew Bach was toying with us, setting up false expectations that he upended when the theme broke off early. This time things went okay, but now the theme split across the hands. You had to avoid getting distracted by the weird homework problems that started to emerge, the invertible counterpoint and its combinatorics.

I got to the first episode, in which Bach snapped off the head of the subject—that *V*-shaped notch—and riffed on it a bit before returning to the subject, but this time in a related key. It always surprised me that the same set of notes with the same set of flats or sharps could be in a different key, just because of the gravitational relationships holding between them; the composer could make one set of tones feel like Ithaka and home, and another like the middle of the ocean. I could feel these relationships of attraction and repulsion being manipulated exquisitely, only for the second episode to appear suddenly before me. What was striking now was how Bach recombined bits and pieces we'd heard previously. There was a beauty in the sheer economy of means, the aesthetic of the plains Indians and the buffalo kill.

My mind began to drift. Was that a hair on the keyboard? Did I have any meetings tomorrow? The blooms on the orchid across the room had unfurled like tiny white sails. My playing generally improved when I daydreamed like this, at least until I arrived at some passage that required executive control over the lizard reflex, and everything came crashing down. I thought about the preceding months. It had felt like cheating to learn this piece before mastering Mozart, but I had come to accept that doing *that* would take much longer, and perhaps I'd never quite succeed. I no longer suffered months being unable to play, but I also didn't have the strength in my right hand to play scales quite right, or practice them enough to do so, whatever I tried. And yet here I was, playing a fugue.

I came to, and saw that we had arrived at the fourth and final episode. In the right hand, the score called for holding down F while playing a separate line that included the same tone. When I had started learning this passage, it had struck me as incredibly painful for the student, almost vindictive on the part of Bach. Why was he torturing us? But that was before I realized that this passage was literally impossible to play, at least in one sense. It was obvious what was loosely intended—you simply had to release and restrike the F a couple of times—but you couldn't actually hold the note down as a drone *and* play over it, as the score seemed to suggest. I developed an elaborate theory according to which the piece was written for an instrument with several manuals, like the Baroque harpsichord, but Christopher pointed out that my theory required the performer to have three arms. (I briefly considered the possibility that Bach *did* have three arms, which would explain a great deal.) You could dismiss those measures as a notational convenience or practical exigency, but I came to see it as Bach trying to demonstrate an almost metaphysical counterpoint that was incapable of being fully realized in flesh and blood, just as his music for solo instruments gestured toward an impossible polyphony. I had to come to appreciate the complete indifference to the petty difficulties of the performer, the prioritization of good music over what it was physically possible to play, and I felt a certain contempt for composers who wrote idiomatically, in thrall to the contingencies of wood and tendon, though Christopher told me this sounded a lot like Stockholm syndrome.

Surprisingly, I still hadn't made a major mistake or broken tempo. This made me much more nervous because now it seemed possible I would actually play the piece through, which had never happened before. I had been thinking and dreaming of this music, BWV 847, for over twenty years, but only in theory and always from the outside, like an observer taking notes, at a third remove from the truth after the performer and the loudspeakers. Now there was a deceptive cadence that I managed not to butcher, and I was knee-deep in the thing, participating for once, not just listening, not just collating. I kept waiting for the piano to make the sound of a puppy dog when you step on its tail, but it didn't happen, and so I trembled, and my forehead bathed in sweat.

The subject entered for the last time, its seventh appearance, resounding deep in the bass as was typical at the conclusion of a fugue. I played this instance long, ignoring the editor's staccato indications, just as I had the initial statement. The piece was pulling to a close, and yet Bach increased the tension still further by landing on some dissonant inverted chords, and then causing the music first to slow, and then to break down altogether, bringing the whole thing to a halt on a rest just a few bars from the finish line, as if he were throwing the race, like some malcontented runner. I thought of two other examples of this: that monumental organ piece, BWV 582, and the opening to *The Art of Fugue*, which ends on a series of dramatic pauses, as if foreshadowing the rupture at the close of the work. At last the music lurched back into motion, and I played the final chord, a *tierce picarde*, like the one that Bach had played at St. Catherine's in Hamburg, and so we ended on the reassuring major.

There was a fermata over that last chord, the dispensation to waive the strict rules of notation and hold the notes as long as you pleased, and so I held on a while, stretching things out and reflecting on the improbable fact that I had somehow managed to stumble through this piece. I was suspicious of my own success. All of this would have to be recorded, verified, and submitted for appraisal, of course. What were the odds that I, who wore flip-flops and T-shirts, who grew up on heavy metal and strip malls, had played some Bach? Still, for just that one moment there was the consciousness that I no longer needed anyone else to play for me, mediated through Wi-Fi and Mylar, for I had become the latest in an endless series of instruments, however imperfect, of Bach's own mind.

6

God

Learning an easy piece like the Fugue in C Minor was an end only to a beginning, or at least what would have been the beginning for a real musician. But even so, there followed a kind of coda that stretched over the ensuing months, as I came to think about the way of Bach as a whole, and what it meant to follow or at least to aspire to following it.

The books about Bach that I read inevitably contained a brief, reluctant treatment of his religion, which the author secretly thought was stupid. And just as my students' papers invariably began, "Since the dawn of time, mankind has pondered life's great questions," or else, "Plato was one of the most famous philosophers of olden days," or perhaps, "The problem of evil begs the question of why there has been the amount of so much suffering," so these books began by saying that Bach lived in a simpler age, an age of faith, an age that found it easy to believe in a divine order of things. And yet the exact opposite was true. The Thirty Years' War was a living memory of mayhem and massacre, religious schism was everywhere, the life expectancy was thirty-five—Bach's wives and children dropped like flies—and the world was an incomprehensible chaos created, as Voltaire wrote at the time, to drive us crazy. It wasn't an age of faith because the world suggested order and harmony; faith alone inspired any confidence in such an order. The world didn't change, we did.

Worse still was Schweitzer's idea that art was Bach's true religion, as if he were some sort of aesthete who was just going through the motions, as if he rolled his eyes and sighed when it was time for one more tedious religious piece. Against this, it was easy enough to point out his *Soli Deo Gloria*'s in the manuscripts—to God alone be the glory—though these were a bit stock for the period, and I found myself more impressed by the eighty-one volumes of theology documented in his library, surely overkill even for a church mouse, or the harrowing examination of his "theological competence" at Leipzig, conducted in Latin, which others failed for not knowing such things as how many chapters there were in each gospel, or where it says, "That is life eternal."[1] Cynics insisted these were all just signs of accommodating Lutheran hierarchy or the fanaticism of the so-called pietists, but as I played and read, I found this hard to believe. For one thing, he didn't really do much accommodating. His church operas—the passions—infuriated the hard-core pietists (to whom Bach really was a decadent aesthete), while his emphasis on deeply personal, emotional involvement with religion—the beating of the breast, the cries of remorse—were more than Lutheran theology suggested; his religious music wasn't a game of examination trivia.[2] But more fundamentally, the music just seemed too *sincere* to me. Nothing could be less pro forma than those multi-hour passions, or, at the other time-scale, the five-note phrases of the stigmata that one finds in *The Goldberg Variations* and the puzzle canons. And mulling all this over, I thought, too, of my own faith and of what had become of it, and of Melville's eternal cycle—from infancy's unconscious spell to disbelief and the pondering repose of IF, and whether playing Bach had merely flipped me back to the beginning of that cycle, and whether the connection I began to see between God and music was more than hocus-pocus.

Tempo: *Langsam und schmachtend*

In the fall, the department assigned me 180 freshmen to teach, with two assistants, who resembled those in Kafka's

Castle. No other faculty were teaching any introductory courses at all—they had assigned the rest to the graduate students, on the paradoxical theory that the students were the better teachers. The undergraduates in turn devised new and innovative ways of tormenting me. They would send me emoji-laden messages from their phones about what they were to read, as if the existence of the syllabus were a great mystery to them; and if they did stumble on the syllabus, they would ask if they *really* needed to get the books it listed for the course; or if they missed class for a few weeks, they would casually ask, "Did we discuss anything *important?*" (Sometimes I experimented with replying "No," to see whether they found that at all surprising, which they did not; at other times I tried a firm "Yes!" which caused them great consternation.) When I returned home I was sometimes too exhausted to play the piano, and I would instead listen to the *St Matthew Passion* or the *Ring* cycle, and ponder Wagner's mockery of Bach, whom, in the course of his anti-Semitic ravings, he called a pedantic formalist who merely pointed the way to Beethoven and himself, the real geniuses.

Superficially, Wagner seemed right, at least in thinking of his music and Bach's as antipodes, even if he was wrong about who came off better. Wagner had more individual genius, but he displayed inferior craftsmanship—the *Ring* is a giant, uncut diamond. It wasn't quite fair to call him "the Puccini of music" (except as a reflection on Puccini) but there was a certain truth in this double-insult. The contrasts were undeniable: the *Passion* is a lugubrious, self-flagellating lament, while the *Ring* is a celebration of vitality and joy, Nietzsche and nature. Who doesn't hear the beginning of *Rheingold* and yearn to sweep away all those cobwebbed tomes of sin and suffering and all the miserable ideas of the past? Both are stories of the superhuman, but Wagner's gods are like Homer's, flawed and anthropomorphic, useful mainly as foils for humanity, not as transcendent ideals. Wagner's notion is that the gods are no more free from the dilemmas and contradictions that their decisions weave for them than are we, since the essential problems of existence are to be found in our choices and our loves, not in limitations on our powers, and so we must seek the answers within. Being a Norse god instead of an area-man can't fix your marriage or pay off the mortgage on Valhalla. Wagner's gods, like Homer's or Camus's, point to a humanism.

But as I listened night after night, the two works started to seem more similar to me than different, and after a few months I concluded that, far from being opposites, the *Passion* and the *Ring* shared the same aesthetic essence, and that what made them seem so different were the diverging philosophies they expressed, not the type of art they represented. For thinking of them only as works of art, both were cosmic in theme and scale, and musically and narratively dense. They were ambitious to the point that neither really can be performed adequately—Bach requires three separate choirs and two orchestras, Wagner

modestly demands 110 instruments, including 18 anvils—
both seemed consummately German since it was impossible to imagine any other country producing or even
wanting to produce these works; their reference-point
was always traditional opera, but with the goal to modify
or exceed it in some way; the music in both was heavily
polyphonic and symbolic, with bizarre mashups of themes
that collided in unexpected ways; and there were leitmo-
tifs threading each of the wholes together. They even
opened similarly, with a drone in the bass expressing the
cosmic background radiation, followed by waves—of
the Rhine in Wagner, or in Bach of tears. Each was the
greatest artist of his age trying to express the meaning of
life as he saw it, just as before them Homer had said that
that meaning was *kleos*, glory, and Plato said it was a type
of knowledge, and Thomas Aquinas said it was Christianity, and Shakespeare that there was no meaning, just a
thousand masks, and the Buddha smiled and said nothing
at all. For Bach the meaning of life wasn't Christianity,
it was Christ; and for Wagner the meaning of life was
Wagner. Or perhaps, more pedantically, it was eros and
ultimately resignation in the face of eros's impossible
union, but this is just another way of saying Wagner. For
he developed his philosophy as a purely personal response
to his own experience, not as a general truth to evangelize
and argue about.

Listening to the choruses at the beginning of the *Passion* came as a great shock after all those fugues, for the

voices were melismatic and singsongy, Venetian taffy to
stretch out the moment, and I wondered if the Italian
captivity was so bad after all, hearing those brusque keyboard angles sanded down to suit the voices. But just when
you thought Bach had sold out to opera, a third group of
singers interrupted, and sang—of all things—a simple
Lutheran hymn that everyone in the audience would have
known. The effect of this irruption cannot be exaggerated.
We seem to have settled nicely into conventional if beautiful choral music, when those unadorned sopranos thrust
themselves into the proceedings with a piercing simplicity.
(Later it reminded me of Debussy's religious procession
emerging out of the mist in *Fêtes*, or his cathedral in the
preludes, breaching off the coast of Brittany.) You were
reminded that this was liturgical music, part of a church
service the audience was participating in, not some
museum piece, and in fact they wouldn't have gotten
the whole thing in one go, but would have heard it in
several parts, separated by an hour or more, as the
interminable service went on and on, the music almost
a novelty since during lent instrumental music was
forbidden.[3] The three choirs duel and surround the
listener on all sides, as the rustic Lutheran tradition of
hymns intersects with concert music, as if to ask whether
it was possible to harmonize not just the various melodies
but the vying traditions and even social purposes of music
itself. (Audiences replied in the negative; no one showed
the slightest interest in this grandiose spectacle or

mentioned it in the papers, and in fact horrified church-goers asked whether this was the beginning of comic operas being performed in the house of God).[4]

To anyone sensitive to the disparate musical forms and traditions on display, the result can seem like a collage, newspaper glued to a painted canvas, a Rembrandt with a background in Florentine blue: it may be glorious but still rather disturbing. On the other hand, I found myself gripped by the primitive in the *Passion* and all its wallowing, despite Wagner's sirens and their impious joys; it was like the procession of San Gennaro in the *Godfather* sequel, where the money pinned to the saint seems in one sense atavistic, but also feels infinitely more sincere than antiseptic lessons from the catechism. And as those peasant hymns anchor themselves into the *Passion*, they begin to lend shape and structure to the three hours, especially "O Haupt voll Blut und Wunden" (O head of blood and wounds), whose melody recurs five times and is obviously supposed to serve as a kind of refrain. In fact, the chorus and chorales begin to take on the role of a Greek chorus, it is often observed, providing an external guide to the action, the ideal spectator's reaction to the events on stage, and by the time the chorus set itself down in tears at the end, I found myself singing along. I ought to have preferred *Rheingold*'s humane vitality, but I found Bach's story of the passion—how different even from Handel's cheerful *Messiah!*—more compelling in the dark nights of the soul when such choices are made, lying awake at night, "O Haupt voll Blut und Wunden" ringing in my ears, at first in D minor and finally in F major.

Even then, another, deeper similarity struck me as I noticed Bach and Wagner's fundamental interest in transformation. This is quite clear in Bach, whose music relies on formal operations like inversion or augmentation, but the leitmotif system in Wagner turned out to be equally complex, to my surprise. There weren't just musical themes associated with characters, objects, or ideas (familiar from movies like *Star Wars*); there were whole families of themes related to one another by musical transformation—an idea steeped in the tradition Bach established. What differed wasn't so much the syntax but the semantics, the meaning of what was being said. For example, the theme associated with Erda—a mysterious, bleak character—derives from the nature motif heard at the opening, but comes in a minor key and varied time signature. And when she prophecies the downfall of the old order ("A dismal day dawns to the gods"), in a passage of piercing beauty, Wagner inverts the rising nature theme to suggest decline, and thus coins the motif for the twilight of the gods.[5] You can practically see them tumbling down from Valhalla. But even then there is more meaning, for the gods will fall in the *major*, for there is joy in resignation; "twilight" doesn't mean the fading of light but "half-light," and points to dawn as much as dusk.

Bach may have thought of Christ and the bureaucracy during the *Passion*, and Wagner of his creditors and of some fake version of Buddhism he got from Schopenhauer, but I felt there was an underlying force they both wielded, that was simply channeled to different ends, and that to really understand the one, you had to understand the other, since otherwise you were liable to miss what was great in each, which had to be worked out by a system of simultaneous equations. The essential lesson of Bach and Wagner was at some level that of the transformation from caterpillar to butterfly, and all great musicians are lepidopterists at heart.

I thought of the many other transformations implied by these works, not just the formal operations on the notes. There was the conversion of the soul in the *Passion*, and the effects of love and power in the *Ring*, and the marvelous complexity achieved by combining transformation with a sense of the return, so that both concluded by depositing us once more on their respective shores, having changed or at least deepened their significance in the interim. And there was the alchemy by which the 17th-century tune, "My Heart is Troubled by a Maiden's Tender Charms" became "O Haupt voll Blut und Wunden," a so-called contrafactum by which the secular was transubstantiated and redeemed, like Johnny Cash singing Depeche Mode's "Personal Jesus," or "Amazing Grace" sung to the tune of "House of the Rising Sun."[6] Of course, there was always the question of what had transformed into what. Was it the tune that survived and altered the meaning of the new words, or did the words alter the meaning of the old tune? Is life fundamentally "Amazing Grace" sung to the tune of "House of the Rising Sun," or is life "House of the Rising Sun" hypocritically sung to the words of "Amazing Grace," I wondered, unable to sleep, or was it both, or some days one and some days the other, all depending?

I decided to try going to church again. This was far more harrowing than I had imagined, a sea of blue hair on hollowed-out pews that closely resembled the audiences at symphony concerts. They were old enough to ask me if I was a student, the way I now had to ask kids whether they were in high school or college, and the hymnals were in large print; at the conclusion of the service they came after me like flesh-eating zombies to fill their empty ranks. Sometimes the hymns were accompanied by synth organ, but in other services there were guitars, or djembe drums or other instruments of those who had replaced the departed, who had been transported by something like an end-time rapture to yoga lessons and nonjudgmental therapy sessions instead of these crumbling temples, which a Babylonian army couldn't have destroyed more thoroughly.

A creed that must be written in large print is already extinct, and eventually I found myself attending Catholic services. I was Protestant, but their type was small and the ritual of the mass ensured that it didn't matter too much what any individual did, or how absurd the homily might be, since you couldn't really screw up kyrie eleison or the Nicene Creed, and Bach's Mass in B Minor seemed to provide a special dispensation to me. At the Protestant services, by contrast, everything depended on the individual, and in practice they tended to devolve into either pop psychology ("God can make you feel better"), or else punishing expositions of the Bible, sprinkled with references to the Greek ("I know more about this stuff than you do"). In general, Catholic services were mostly about God, while Protestant services were mostly about the pastor and his dream of the ten-part series on Pauline eschatology that he yearned to deliver and his flock dreaded to hear. But at least the Catholic services didn't last four hours, I didn't have to rent or buy a pew, and there was no rabble standing in the back as the rich enjoyed their heated chapels, as in Bach's day.

Drifting during the homily, I thought of the five wounds of Christ and the five *Wunden* chorales, of the twelve tones of the octave and the twelve tribes of Israel and the twelve apostles, of the three voices of my fugue, the three persons of the trinity, the three times Peter denied Christ, the three times Paul begged God to remove the thorn from his side and the three times God refused, of his three shipwrecks and the three times Odysseus tried to grasp the ghost of my mother, of the willing spirit and the weak flesh, and Paul's thorn and my broken hands, and I started to feel I should have been trying to become worthy of playing Bach, rather than trying to conquer the notes, and that the main reason I couldn't play anything properly was that I lacked an Augustinian theory of the piano and a postlapsarian technique—what I needed wasn't practice, the works of the flesh, but grace, and that would be sufficient. (The priest seemed to be discussing his old car as a metaphor for something or other, and gesticulated toward the wall with a fervid intensity.) I thought, too, of the sadness of playing music alone, when it was intended to bring us together, and how the piano lets you cheat by simulating the orchestra and avoiding the other players, a kind of musical pornography. I thought of the greatness to which we're called, and the insignificance we accept. I resolved to repent and play better, but above all to live better, to drink less, to call home more, and play in a band.

The obvious nexus between Bach's music and God were works like the *St Matthew Passion*, but I had noticed that many claimed a deeper connection between music and God's creation, and ultimately to God himself. When I taught my students about Plato, for instance, I was reminded of his two great inspirations—his teacher Socrates, and the Pythagoreans of Italy, who were obsessed with the mathematics behind music, and more broadly with number as a guide to reality (as well as reincarnation and avoiding beans at all costs). This began with their discovery of the proportions' underlying intervals, so that a length of string twice as long sounds an octave higher, a ratio of 3:2 produces a perfect fifth interval, and so on, and culminated in theories of the music of the heavenly spheres that were supposed to contain the stars put in place by the gods. And Plato himself said that the universe had a soul composed according to the Dorian mode, the cosmos having an order that mirrors the rational order of our own minds, as expressed in music or in the harmony of the ideal city of the *Republic*. (Sadly, the part about the musical spheres was later refuted by Aristotle, who pointed out that when you listen really carefully you can't actually hear anything.)

I felt a superficial attraction to this idea of connecting music and number. Certainly, my own musical life had boiled down to a series of numbers: there was BWV 847, my beloved lodestar; there was the 244 of the *Passion*; then 542 and 582 for the organ; and finally BWV 1080 for *The Art of Fugue*, the dead man's hand; then Glenn Gould's unlucky pianos, CD 174 and 318; Mozart's K. 545 for beginners, and then his own dead man's hand of 626, the *Requiem*. Musical connoisseurs who didn't share a language could spend an evening simply writing these numbers down on a napkin and exchanging knowing smiles and the occasional tear.

Later, the Pythagorean ideas were revived by Galileo and Kepler, like a conversation briefly interrupted by 2000 years of mediocrity. They proposed that even number-worshiping Pythagoreans should do some experiments and make some observations, for even if reality was scripted in mathematics, visible only to blind reason, our knowledge of it could be facilitated by looking around. It's a mistake, though, to picture Kepler as some pious devotee of data, like a renaissance PhD, when his books are bestiaries of astrology, geometry, theology, astronomy, and most importantly, music. Discovering the elliptical shape of the orbits and the laws of planetary motion was only a small part of his ambition; what he really wanted was to explain how those movements revealed the hand of God. The orbits of the planets were to fit inside spheres placed between the Platonic solids of the Lutheran demiurge; Mars sounded a perfect fifth in the ratio of his speeds at perihelion and aphelion, as if God were composing by the motions of the heavens. Of course, all of this was madness, and if it weren't for Newton we'd hardly believe in Kepler's laws at all.

It was the 19th-century philosopher Schopenhauer who took this mania furthest. He claimed that music was an expression of "the things in themselves," or what he called "the Will," which in the European manner of philosophy he rigorously declined to explain across twenty-five years and fifteen hundred pages. (He is nevertheless regarded as a model of lucidity because his rival Hegel, whom he despised, was even more obscure.) In fact, Schopenhauer's work contained such inscrutable rambling that it soon attracted the attention of Wagner, who recognized a kindred spirit and might have struck up a friendship had Schopenhauer not decided that Rossini (!) was the real genius of the opera. The general idea, in any case, seems to have been that music needn't be representational the way the visual arts are, at least not of the objects around us, and that this makes music special and in some sense superior. A painting of a French bar is a copy or representation of one; Plato, who thought that the things in this world are faint copies of eternal archetypes, would have said the painting is at a third remove from the truth. Music, by contrast, was supposed to connect us to reality itself. A fugue isn't a copy of anything, and since music aptly conveys drives and urges it was simple enough for Schopenhauer to connect this idea to his mysterious talk of the Will. But superficial Americans will wonder what a placid chant succeeds in representing in this scheme, and ultimately there is as little sense to be made of all this as there is of Kepler's bestiary.

I left behind Schopenhauer's Will and Kepler's Platonic solids without feeling I had made much progress. These speculations were like expeditions to remote peaks from which no one ever returned, or like Kant's dove, which thought that if it was easy to fly in the light air, it would be easier still to fly through space. The truth seemed to me after a while both simpler and more complicated. The Pythagorean impulse was to think not just that mathematics explained or described the world, but that there was a hidden world *behind* the world, invisible, mathematical, and apprehensible only through reason. But what the Pythagoreans had really discovered was only that our *descriptions* of the world must be written in mathematics to be tolerably precise and informative, and that this language could be used to describe our music, as well. The cosmos itself doesn't exemplify any striking mathematical order—a fact that should have seemed obvious to the Pythagoreans once they recognized the irrational numbers, which, contrary to their expectations, cannot be expressed as a ratio between whole numbers. (Those who didn't keep the secret are said to have been banished, and the one who discovered it drowned by the gods in punishment.) On the contrary, the mathematics that describes the universe is full of inelegant constants and random gibberish, as if everything had to be tuned or tempered by hand, hammered and shoved into place the night before the science project was due. We forget this because mathematics itself is elegant, but of course it is—it reflects the cosmos of our own minds. The planets themselves don't fit between the Platonic solids; their orbits don't correspond to diatonic scales or whole number ratios. The earth's orbit is basically a circle, but with just enough eccentricity to drive us crazy; the world could have been a tetrahedron or a perfect sphere, but it isn't. The world isn't musical, but then music itself isn't perfectly rational either, and the cosmos at the keyboard must itself be tempered as Bach himself proved so forcefully.

Still, there *was* something right in all this—in the quest for the meaning of music and its connection to God, in the idea that music involves the soul doing hidden or occult arithmetic, as Leibniz put it, that it contains "unconscious congruences." The mistake lay in trying to make all this about the world instead of our own minds. Music harnesses the autonomic systems of tension and release that register the drama in a baby's cry, in finding a parking space or approaching a precipice, in seeing a car swerve toward us, in seeing virtue rewarded or the innocent punished, in all the value and disvalue around us that the emotions make us perceive. We are conscious beings for whom life has emotional *tone*, for whom each day is a series of minor triumphs and disasters involving a million subtle discriminations, and music activates this drama. Each little phrase from low to high, each dissonant interval, or subverted expectation, mimics the human comedy and sets our bodies aflicker. Music gets at what we are at the deepest level; only beings like us can participate in the drama of music and reflect on all the associations and reverberations it sets off. And because music hijacks our glands and our spinal cords, not just the prefrontal cortex, it is reptilian in a way that painting and literature are not. Music is like a drug that interfaces directly with the nervous system, while the other arts must labor through the formal channels, with passport controls and customs inspections. We reject a novel with the wrong politics, but the devil can convert the saint against his will with the right record, which is why Plato banned the electric guitar. (It is strange that we are visual creatures as measured by brain-volume, but moved so much more by sound.)

You could see all this in just the major and minor chords. When the light had faded, I would sit at the piano and play the perfect interval C and G, and then add either the E or E flat in the middle for a major or minor chord, like Bach playing the *tierce picarde* in Hamburg. I would switch back and forth, or try playing a loud E first, and then add the G, and then only add the C softly at the end. But whatever I tried, the mysterious difference remained: the one connoted a world of sadness and failure, the other of triumph and virtue. But why? Both chords contained the same ingredients, a major and a minor third, and the result was the same whichever notes you emphasized. Why did this tiny difference of a semitone produce such a strong reaction on our autonomic systems of assessment? The philosophers and musicologists were divided between two wrong theories. The one group insisted that we had all been brainwashed into merely *imagining* this difference between the major and the minor, which they proved by showing that somewhere there were some pygmies who didn't cry listening to the Cure. We were to suppose that in an alternate history the conventions would have made Pink Floyd sound cheerful, which was like saying that people want to eat sugar because of advertising by the sugar lobby. The other group insisted, more profoundly, that the distinction was to be found in the tones themselves, perhaps because the major triad contains tones that sound more natural, since they can be found earlier in the harmonic series—those natural resonances that sound softly above the fundamental when a string vibrates—or because the overtones of the notes in the major clash less with one another than those of the minor. This, too, seemed strained though, since many nice sounding chords have clashing overtones, and in the end, I added this to the many mysteries of Bach I had accumulated.

The Pythagoreans were obsessed with harmony but strangely uninterested in the temporal aspect of music. (Why didn't Kepler associate the planetary orbits with rhythm, one wants to know, especially since he was so focused on their angular *velocities*?) And yet music is harmony in time. Music coordinates two dimensions of our existence—our momentary consciousness of value that gives shape to our inner lives, and our experience as temporal and thus finite beings. God sees all of eternity, not being subject to time's passage, while we fly through time's narrow tube like a paranoid mole racing through his burrow. I listened to the metronome, always a bit ahead of me, just out of reach as I worked on my Bach. God, I imagined, grasps the score of history all at once, taking in the whole, while we live on the point of the baton intoning each separate note as it occurs. There were those who said that time's passage was an illusion, but I found that impossible to believe, sitting there listening to the lashes of the metronome. There was the perspective from outside of time, shared by God and the laws of nature, which make no reference to a shimmering NOW that glides on by, any more than does the musical score. But it was still true that I had not yet played the final chord—not just that it occurred *later*, but that I hadn't reached it *yet*. It was as if one were to pretend that there were only musical scores and no performances of them.

From one point of view, then, music is disappointing, since it says nothing and is the least articulate of the arts—at its most pure it isn't about anything and refers no further than itself. From this perspective, music is a mere afterglow of the mind, the useless heat of the incandescent bulb, and the Pythagorean in us regrets it all and wishes that music really did unlock the secret order of the cosmos. But in another sense music is mankind's highest calling, touching on all that is riddle and glory in us, conscious beings shackled in time. Music, I concluded, exists to praise the work of creation. Not because harmony reflects the mathematics of nature, but because it reflects our own consciousness as dramas of choice and chance, the fundamental miracle that we are machines, atoms held together by belts and pulleys, bound by time and law, and yet a little less than angels. And in our conscious caring we share in the divine, which is what it means to say that we are made in the image of God. Music isn't representational, and therefore cannot make idolatrous pictures of Him, any more than one of us can resemble Him. But for that very reason, music is the true face of God.

After these arduous and perhaps quixotic ascents, I felt relief getting back to Bach himself, and contemplating his way and why, after all, I felt such an affinity with him—when I had discovered that the distance between us was so very vast once you accounted for his craftsmanship and how different his time and place were from my suburbs. And despite all the numerology, it was the visual side of Bach that brought out these differences most clearly, at a time when I imagined I already knew a great deal about him. For I had never yet studied his autograph scores apart from the scribblings in Anna's notebook, and after three years I thought I should do so, just in case there was something to be learned from his way of writing out the Fugue in C Minor. I obtained a facsimile of the first book of *The Well-Tempered Clavier* in Bach's fair copy, and immediately saw that it was comparable to illuminated manuscripts like the Book of Kells. Or better still, his written music resembled Japanese art or calligraphy, pines in an ink wash, or the sweeping curves of *shodo* characters, that have to be produced both rapidly and precisely to convey both spontaneity and perfection.

The great whoosh of ink, for instance, connecting the F in measure 7 with the soprano notes above seemed like it had been produced on a tatami mat, sitting cross-legged with one hand holding the sleeve of the other to prevent a stain. The writing of Mozart, by contrast, was an over-delicate pointilism, not to speak of Beethoven's mess of mistakes and inkblots, which really were grotesque.

Lauren pointed out a certain feminine quality in Bach's hand, or perhaps, we decided, it was better described as a Taoist element, the way in certain styles of kung fu (or at least in certain Jackie Chan movies) one doesn't resist the punches so much as smoothly flex with them, and victory comes by softness and weakness. Glenn Gould's playing seemed hypermasculine, or perhaps a bit rigid, in light of this notation, which was firm but supple, flexible like bamboo. There was order and precision (the staves were ruled), but combined with whimsy and laughter (the bar lines were not). I thought of the fronds of seaweed, of my ceaseless efforts to attain a sea change in my fingers, and felt encouraged, even if the goal was shrouded in mist. It was the writing of a supremely confident sage who no longer had to try, who told the devotees who climbed the thousands of steps to his hut, when they complained that their years of suffering still had not endowed them with the success they sought, that his only secret was that he never tried at all.

Never did I feel closer to Bach, or further away, than looking at his own hand, after all these years. How could my playing possibly be worthy of that whooshing F? Sometimes it seemed as if Bach had been sent to us so that no one would have anything to brag about again, the difference between him and the rest of us, as encoded in those autographs, being so utterly alienating.

❧

Comme un tendre et triste regret

Surveying all the bits and pieces of Bach I had accumulated over the years, I felt more American than ever, despite having lived a hundred miles from his house for a while. I cringed at Schopenhauer's jokes and Bach's quest for titles; I felt transfigured at Walden Pond. We are too distracted to produce anything like Bach, but then we have Venice Beach and rock 'n' roll, while they have *Freizeitgestaltungsmöglichkeiten* (freetimestructuringpossibilities). No one could have loved this music more, but I remained a blundering American brought up on grape soda and hair bands, now more than ever.

I felt American playing Bach in the same way I felt reading the later novels of Henry James, the ones you pick up with enthusiasm and set down again, spent, after a few paragraphs. (Lauren was the only person I knew who read, let alone enjoyed them.) The characters shipped off to Europe, vulgar, meretricious, capable of buying art but not really of understanding it, grown rich by manufacturing some article too embarrassing to name outright, and faced off against Europeans who had infinitely more refined perceptions. Or so it seemed. The fun of it was trying to decide whether the clumsy Americans harbored a shrewd wisdom beneath it all, whether the simplicity of a Milly Theale was a weapon no sophistication could withstand, or whether Europe offered a kind of liberty you couldn't find in America despite the stereotypes. (In the end, the Americans won 3–0 by novels, but perhaps only because the triumph of simplicity is the more interesting story to tell.)

With James as ambassador, I even made sporadic forays into understanding the French approach, even more alien to me. I could never pray to the false gods of Ravel, or Debussy and his ridiculous performance indications that rivaled Bach's letters in their absurdity, nor wholly approve his talent for getting women to shoot themselves, but I could at least admire the temple they had constructed, which I imagined submerged and made of stone and colored glass, with opalescent fish drifting amid the buttresses and triforium. If Bach had sought to extend himself by assimilating parts of Italy and France, shouldn't we try to do the same? I tiptoed after Debussy's footsteps in the snow; I visited his sunken cathedral, awed by the originality and the fineness of perception. And even in the arena of pop culture, who can watch *The Umbrellas of Cherbourg* without feeling a little ashamed not to be French? So Bach's attempts at universality, which I'd resented despite what all the scholars said, lured me outward and away from prejudice.

James was the true chronicler of the Revolutionary War, of which Yorktown was the opening skirmish, and whose roles of colony and colonizer were always in flux. The Genius of the West was born in Egypt and Mesopotamia, then drifted ever north and west through Greece and Italy, then northwestern Europe (with a brief stop in Eisenach); then it made its leap to the New World, and finally lit upon LA and Silicon Valley, where it wobbles precariously, in search of welcome shores. But the contest for independence went and still goes back and forth, across food, art, and industry, Marshall's Cold War cradle, the Internet, and on and on. ("The Yankees have colonized our subconscious," says the director Wim Wenders, as if pizza and the Eiffel Tower didn't count.) At their worst, America is Disneyland and kitsch, and Europe a museum, a kind of intellectual taxidermy. The pianist Zhu Xiao-Mei says that labor camp was tough but nothing compared to the mental tortures of Disney, while any American in Europe knows that the museum culture, the passion for stasis and stamps in books, can be tough, as well.

Despite all this, I felt that an inexplicable connection with Bach remained. Perhaps it was the very improbability of discovering and liking him in the first place so many years ago, fumbling through my parents' record collection and seeing Gould's face between Kenny Rogers and *16 ABBA Hits*, across from the bookcase full of *Reader's Digests* and *Guideposts*. No one in the world could have been less predisposed to this music. In that sense, playing the piano in my suburban study seemed every bit as incongruous as Albert Schweitzer playing Bach in the jungle or Zhu learning Bach in the refrigerator of a Chinese labor camp. To connect with Bach across such vast distances—distances that the novels of Henry James serve to measure as if by a sextant—was precisely what made the affinity so meaningful.

Apart from my father and brother, Bach was the oldest thing I'd continuously cared about, my oldest friend, a life-metronome. There wasn't some neat lesson to be learned in all this, a slogan to put on a T-shirt. But I felt now an attraction to a particular set of ideas, and no matter how far I drifted, I could recognize them by the sense of return once I stumbled home. If I couldn't whoosh across the keyboard and flex like bamboo, I had become subject to a certain kind of gravity. I sought out the virtues of imperfection; I prized craftsmanship above all else and I despised genius, the lazy man's art; I admired arrogance in the conception and humility in the execution; I looked down on noisy gestures and sought meaning in mere passing tones; I looked for transformations and transpositions that suggested all we should transform in ourselves; and I was cynical about the bureaucracy but naïve toward friends and all they had to teach and learn from us. I, too, tottered under the disco ball; I lacked French grace and Italian panache; I, too, crumpled at the hand of the opposer. But what connected me to Bach in the end wasn't any similarity, much less ability, but a shared ideal he burnished, a common impression of God and good.

My body was not my body, I had learned. It was an ensemble loosely under my command, but full of free agents and minor rebellions, worn-out parts and defectors. The intervals between Wittgenstein days grew ever greater, but something felt more or less always off, a weakness or aching that never really went away, and I remained incapable of typing or using a camera for more than a few minutes. But it didn't matter. I had imagined that eventually there would be some ribbon I'd break to gentle applause, but of course that had always been silly; there was only the endless march forward, the loneliness of the long distance runner. There was a perverse, existential joy in having a fixed direction but no terminus.

Nor did I ever learn to play with others, perhaps the whole point of music in the first place. There was no band; I drank more, not less, sitting alone at the keyboard at night. Music connects: moment to moment by melody, note to note by chords, movement to movement, person to person—but how? But even that didn't matter. I thought of Lauren who sat through all sixteen hours of the Ring cycle with me and developed a theory of the boring as a result, who had taught me the smell of mimosa flowers and of walnut leaves. (When I looked left into the fallboard there was now a faint glimmer, a hoop of gold kindling in the dark like the Nibelung hoard.) Someday I would play a few bars for her and she would make us tea, and that was enough. I thought, too, of Mother and of the longing for home, however unreal or gilded by desire, of her cabbage, of Bach and Odysseus's dream of completing some impossible cycle, not as rivers return to the sea, but more violently, like fishes struggling upstream, until one day we arrive at the final stretto, when the subject enters more and more insistently, overlapping with itself like waves crashing against the shore, and the pedal point sounds deep in the bass, a low, whooshing F, and the cadential harmony looms across the bars that race forward like the shoreline, and at last the final chord sounds, a colossal F major voiced clear across the keyboard, may it sustain forever in the divine fermata, world without end.

Glossary

Alberti bass—A piano motif in the left hand that consists of outlining the notes to a chord repeatedly.

Arpeggio—The notes of a chord sounded consecutively instead of simultaneously. A broken chord.

Augmentation—The adjustment of note values in a theme to make it last longer and sound as if it were playing in slow motion.

Cadence—The conclusion to a musical passage or piece. Sometimes "deceptive" in virtue of promising a conclusion that doesn't appear.

Canon—A musical form in which each voice precisely imitates the one before it.

Cantabile—In a smooth and vocal-like style.

Chord—A group of notes sounded together, usually three or more.

Counterpoint—Music conceived of as overlapping melodies rather than sequences of chords.

Dynamics—The loudness or softness of music, which instruments like the harpsichord generally cannot render.

Fermata—An instruction to hold and extend a note at the performer's discretion.

Figured bass—A system of music in which the composer indicates the harmonic structure in shorthand, along with melodic contours, which provides a blueprint the performer is expected to realize by improvisation.

Henry James—A device for measuring cultural distance, usually across the Atlantic. Forbidding and difficult, no one should attempt Henry James alone.

Homophonic—A musical texture emphasizing a single melody that is supported by vertical harmony.

Interval—The inclusive distance between two notes. (The distance between C and G is a fifth.)

Inversion—A procedure for producing the mirror image of an original theme, so that where the original rises in pitch the inversion goes down, and vice versa.

Melisma—The practice of teasing several notes out of a single syllable, usually a vowel.

Mode—A system for dividing the octave into fixed steps, e.g., the major scale or the Dorian mode.

Monody—A musical style with a clear, single vocal line and accompaniment, characteristic of the early Baroque and unlike the polyphony of the Renaissance.

Octave—The musical interval between one pitch and another with twice its frequency, e.g., from C to the next higher C.

Ostinato—A brief, repeated musical figure or pattern. Italian for "obstinate, stubborn."

Pedal point—A note held in the bass that persists as a drone, while the rest of the music moves forward.

Piano—From fortepiano ("loud and soft"), marking the fact that the precursors to the piano couldn't implement such dynamics. Authentic period performances that feature the harpsichord mostly lack the contrast between loud and soft.

Polyphony—In general, a musical texture in which there are overlapping voices that move independently. Sometimes the term is more specifically associated with the techniques of Renaissance composers like Palestrina in contrast to the counterpoint of the Baroque.

Retrograde motion—Backward motion in which the notes of a melody are played in reverse.

Scale—A series of notes dividing the octave that define a key signature, e.g., the C major scale.

Staccato—Playing the notes in a punctuated, detached fashion. The opposite of a legato style in which the notes are smoothly joined.

Step—A measure of musical distance or interval. A half step is the interval from any black key on the piano to the adjacent white key, or a minor second. A whole step is an interval of a major second, or the distance between any two white keys separated by a black key on the piano.

Stretto—The overlapping of the subject of a fugue with itself, so that the "answer" to the subject is heard before the subject has been fully stated.

Temperament—The tuning of an instrument whereby the purity of some intervals is compromised in order to extend the range of intervals (and keys) that sound acceptable.

Tierce picarde—A major chord that concludes a piece in a minor key.

Timbre—The character of sound that distinguishes, e.g., a piano from a trumpet playing the same note.

Trill—The rapid alternation between two notes, frequently serving as an ornament in Baroque music.

Voice—A melodic line or part in a piece of music.

Wolf interval—An especially dissonant fifth interval that arises in some tuning systems, which well-temperament is designed to eliminate.

Works Cited

Cantagrel, Gilles. *J.-S. Bach—L'Oeuvre Instrumentale*. Paris: Buchet/Chastel, 2018.

Cooke, Deryck. *Wagner: An Introduction to Der Ring des Nibelungen*. Sound recording. Decca, 1968.

Gaines, James. *Evening in the Palace of Reason: Bach Meets Frederick the Great in the Age of Enlightenment*. New York: Harper, 2005.

Gardiner, John Eliot. *Bach: Music in the Castle of Heaven*. New York: Knopf, 2013.

Geck, Martin. *Johann Sebastian Bach: Life and Work*. San Diego: Harcourt, 2006.

Greenberg, Robert. *Bach and the High Baroque*. Chantilly, Va.: The Great Courses, 1998.

Hafner, Katie. *A Romance on Three Legs*. London: Bloomsbury, 2008.

Lehman, Bradley. "Bach's Extraordinary Temperament: Our Rosetta Stone." *Early Music* (2005) 33 (1): 3–23.

Milka, Anatoly. *Rethinking J. S. Bach's The Art of Fugue.* Abingdon, UK: Routledge, 2016.

Pelikan, Jaroslav. *Bach Among the Theologians.* Eugene, Ore.:Wipf and Stock, 2003.

Platen, Emil. *Die Matthäus-Passion von Johann Sebastian Bach.* Kassel, Germany: DTV/Bärenreiter, 1991.

Rathey, Markus. *Bach's Major Vocal Works.* New Haven, Conn.: Yale University Press, 2016.

Schweitzer, Albert. *J. S. Bach*, Vols. I–II. Mineola, N.Y.: Dover, 1966.

Smith, Timothy. "That 'Crown of Thorns.'" *Bach* 28 (1997) 144–150.

Spalding, Almut and Paul Spalding. *The Account Books of the Reimarus Family of Hamburg, 1728–1780: Turf and Tailors, Books and Beer.* Leiden, Netherlands: Brill, 2015.

Spitta, Philipp. *Johan Sebastian Bach*, Vols. I–III. New York: Dover, 1979.

Wagner, Richard. *Das Judentum in der Musik*. Frankfurt, Germany: Klaus Fischer Verlag, 2010.

Wolff, Christoph, Hans T. David, and Arthur Mendel. *The New Bach Reader*. New York: W.W. Norton, 1998.

Wolff, Christoph. *Bach: Essays on His Life and Music*. Cambridge, Mass.: Harvard University Press, 1994.

———. *Johann Sebastian Bach: The Learned Musician*. New York: W.W. Norton, 2001.

Yearsley, David. *Bach and the Meanings of Counterpoint*. Cambridge, UK: Cambridge University Press, 2002.

Zhu, Xiao-Mei. *The Secret Piano*. Seattle: Amazon Crossing, 2012.

Endnotes

FOUR: THE MAN

1   Wolff, David, and Mendel, 1998, 118–119.
2   Wolff, David, and Mendel, 1998, 325.
3   Wagner 2010, 55–56. Cp. Schweitzer 1966 II, 50ff.
4   Schopenhauer, 2011, 104.
5   Wolff, 2000, 421.
6   Gardiner, 2013, 204.
7   Wolff, David, and Mendel, 1998, 172–185.
8   Yearsley, 2002, ch. 2.
9   Smith, 1997. The related points below are likewise from Smith. See also Smith's website, especially http://www2.nau.edu/tas3/wtc/sdg.html, accessed 1/12/2018. Cp. Cantagrel, 2018, 421–422.
10 Lehman, 2005.
11 Wolff, 1994, ch. 19.
12 Milka, 2017, 221ff.

FIVE: THE PIANO

1   Spitta, 1979, vol. II, 16.
2   Wolff, David, and Mendel, 1998, 90.
3   See Spalding and Spalding, 2015. vol.1, 50.
4   Hafner, 2008.

SIX: GOD

1   Geck, 2006, 132.
2   Pelikan, 2003, 61.
3   Rathey, 2016, 109–110.
4   Platen, 1991, 214.
5   Cooke, 1968.
6   Greenberg, 1998, 207.